MW00764215

ANSYS®Workbench™ Tutorial

Structural & Thermal Analysis using the ANSYS Workbench Release 13 Environment

Kent L. Lawrence

Mechanical and Aerospace Engineering
University of Texas at Arlington

ISBN: 978-1-58503-671-4

PUBLICATIONS

Schroff Development Corporation

www.SDCpublications.com

Kent L. Lawrence is Professor of Mechanical and Aerospace Engineering, University of Texas at Arlington where he has served as Graduate Advisor, Chair of the Department, and supervised the graduate work of over one hundred masters and PhD students. He is a Life Fellow of ASME, the author of the books *ANSYS Tutorial*, SDC Publications, *ANSYS Workbench Tutorial*, SDC Publications and coauthor with Robert L. Woods of the text *Modeling and Simulation of Dynamic Systems*, Prentice-Hall.

Dedicated to:

CABL, always there and always an inspiration,

and

James H. Lawrence, Jr., the family's first engineer.

PREFACE

The exercises in the **ANSYS Workbench Tutorial** introduce the reader to effective engineering problem solving through the use of this powerful modeling, simulation and optimization tool. Topics covered include solid modeling, stress analysis, conduction/convection heat transfer, thermal stress, natural frequencies and elastic buckling. The book is designed for practicing and student engineers alike and is suitable for use with an organized course of instruction or for self-study.

The ANSYS Inc. Finite Element Method (FEM) software is one of the most mature, widely distributed and popular commercial and academic computer aided engineering (CAE) programs available. The ANSYS Workbench environment provides the user with a powerful, intuitive alternative to the "classic" or "traditional" ANSYS APDL GUI.

I am most appreciative of the continued support of research and teaching efforts in our universities provided by ANSYS, Inc and for the encouragement to pursue this project given by Paul Lethbridge of ANSYS.

Heartfelt thanks go to Prof. Dereje Agonafer, ever a supporter of this effort, who together with Mukund Narasimhan, Ajay Menon, Abhijit Kaisare, Saeed Ghalambor and Thiagarajen Raman provided helpful examples, comments, and suggestions for use with this and earlier versions of the software.

Stephen Schroff of SDC Publications urged me to try the tutorial approach in class with the Roger Toogood Pro/E Tutorial book and has been very helpful to me in the preparation of the ANSYS related materials. To Stephen I am most indebted as well as to Ms. Mary Schmidt of SDC for her careful assistance with the manuscript. Hats off also to the University of Alberta group for setting the bar for tutorial standards.

Special thanks go as usual to Carol Lawrence, ever supportive and always willing to proof even the most arcane and cryptic stuff.

The tutorials/exercises in this book can be completed by users with access to the ANSYS Inc. release 13.0 product that contains ANSYS structural & thermal capability together with ANSYS Design Modeler or an alternate solid modeler such as Pro/E, CATIA, SolidWorks, etc.

Please feel free to point out any problems that you may notice with the tutorials in this book. Your comments are welcome at **lawrence@uta.edu** and can only help to improve what is presented here. Additions and corrections to the book will be posted on **mae.uta.edu/~lawrence/ANSYSWBtutorial**, so please check there for any errata to the version that you are using.

Kent L. Lawrence

CONTENTS

INTRODUCTION

CHAPTER 1 – SOLID MODELING FUNDAMENTALS

CHAPTER 2 – PLACED FEATURES, ASSEMBLY

CHAPTER 3 – MODELING TECHNIQUES

CHAPTER 4 – ANSYS MECHANICAL I

CHAPTER 5 - ANSYS MECHANICAL II

CHAPTER 6 – WIZARDS & TOOLS

CHAPTER 7 – HEAT TRANSFER & THERMAL STRESS

CHAPTER 8 – SURFACE & LINE MODELS

LESSON 9 – NATURAL FREQUENCIES & BUCKLING LOADS

REFERENCES

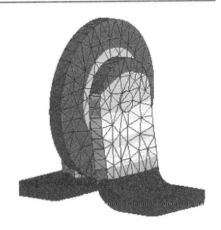

Introduction

I-1   OVERVIEW

Engineers routinely use **Solid Modelers** together with the **Finite Element Method (FEM)** to solve everyday problems of **modeling** for **form/fit/function, stress, deformation, heat transfer, fluid flow, electromagnetics**, etc. using commercial as well as special purpose computer codes. This book presents a collection of tutorials for **ANSYS Workbench**, one of the most versatile and widely used of the commercial solid modeling, simulation and optimization programs.

The tutorials discuss in turn solid modeling, stress analysis, conduction/convection heat transfer, thermal stress, vibration and buckling. Mesh creation and adjustment as well as transferring models from CAD solid modelers are also included.

The tutorials progress from simple to complex. Since, each tutorial can be mastered in a short period of time, the entire book quickly provides a complete, basic introduction to the concepts and capabilities of the extensive ANSYS Workbench software suite.

I-2   THE PROCESS

The part/product analysis process can be divided into three distinct phases

1. **SOLID MODELING** – Build a digital representation of the part/system.

2. **SIMULATION** – Apply materials, loads and constraints; specify the analysis type; determine response quantities.

3. **OPTIMIZATION** – Determine optimum settings for the parameters that control the design.

The execution of these three steps is conveniently encapsulated in the ANSYS Workbench environment as we shall see in the chapter tutorials that follow.

I-3   THE TUTORIALS

A short description of each of the ANSYS Workbench Tutorials follows.

Chapter 1 - Solid Modeling Fundamentals- A simple cross section is used to introduce basic solid modeling concepts with ANSYS DesignModeler by extruding, revolving and sweeping the section.

Chapter 2 - Placed Features, Assembly – This chapter covers creation of features whose shape is predetermined. Among these are: Holes, Rounds, Chamfers, and Patterns. A simple assembly modeling exercise is also included.

Chapter 3 – Modeling Techniques – Examples include modeling techniques that illustrate the flexibility inherent in the feature-based parametric modeling of DesignModeler We consider the use of Parameters, other CAD systems, as well as Surface and Line models.

Chapter 4 – ANSYS Mechanical I - In this Chapter we consider stress response of a plate with a central hole, stress response to various FEM mesh densities, and the use of convergence criteria for controlling solution accuracy.

Chapter 5 – ANSYS Mechanical II - This chapter covers stress and deflection simulation response of some three-dimensional solids representative of typical mechanical parts. We consider the simulation of a Pressure Vessel, an Angle Bracket, and a Clevis Yoke.

Chapter 6 – Wizards & Tools - ANSYS Simulation provides a number of Tools and Wizards to assist with successful simulation projects. This chapter illustrates the use of these in typical applications. In particular we discuss the use of Wizards for simulation problem setup and Tools for simulation result assessment.

Chapter 7 – Heat Transfer & Thermal Stress - In this chapter we demonstrate the use of ANSYS Mechanical for determining temperature distributions for conduction/convection problems and subsequently employing temperature distributions to find thermal stresses.

Chapter 8 – Surface & Line Models – Discussed here are structural and thermal simulation response problems that can be analyzed with surface models or with line models. These include: Plane Stress, Plane Strain or Axisymmetric problems, Plate (shell) problems, as well as Line-body (beam element) problems.

Chapter 9 – Natural Frequencies & Buckling Loads - In this Chapter we discuss the use of ANSYS Mechanical to determine the natural frequencies and normal modes of structural parts and systems. The determination of buckling load estimates for such objects is also covered. In particular we illustrate the determination of Natural Frequencies, corresponding Mode Shapes, and Buckling Load estimates.

The chapters are necessarily of varying length and can be worked through from start to finish. Those with previous ANSYS Workbench experience may want to skip around a bit as needs and interests dictate. Also note that a solid modeler other than DesignModeler can be used in many of the tutorials.

I-4 THE ANSYS Workbench INTERFACE

To start, select **ANSYS 12.1 > Workbench** from the Windows Programs list as shown in Figure I-1 below.

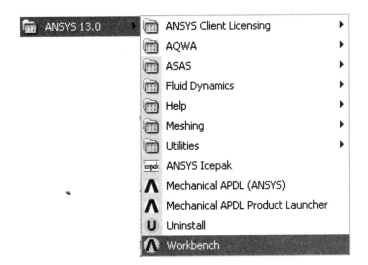

Figure I-1 Start ANSYS Workbench.

(Here we're using 12.1, but these tutorials function equally under 12.0)
Following the splash page, the Workbench interface of Figure I-2 appears. This is the main project page from which we'll do most of our work.

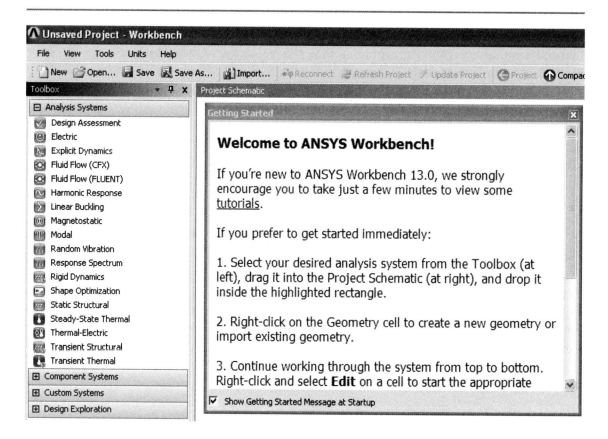

Figure I-2 ANSYS Workbench Project interface.

The information box 'Welcome to ANSYS Workbench' provides links to tutorials as well as an outline of steps to take if you want to go to work immediately. Uncheck the box at the bottom to suppress this message in future start ups.

The Analysis Systems menu in the upper left corner contains options for Electric (ANSYS), Explicit Dynamics (ANSYS), Fluid Flow (CFX), etc., eighteen options in all. This menu is shown in Figure I-3 next.

To open one of the **Analysis System Modules**, **double click** on the desired option or select it and **drag it to the right** into the **Project Schematic** section of the workspace.

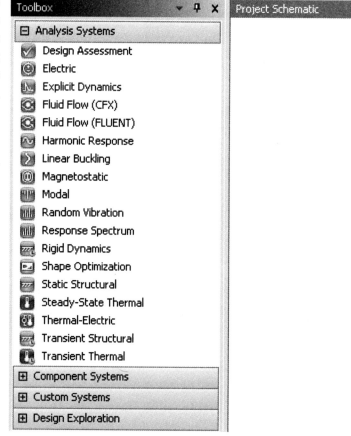

Figure I-3 Analysis system options.

Expand the **Component Systems**, **Custom Systems**, and **Design Exploration** boxes to display additional analysis choices.

Figure I-4 shows the additional options available, and under Component Systems, the **Design Modeler (DM) Geometry** module is highlighted; it is the module we will use in the next chapter.

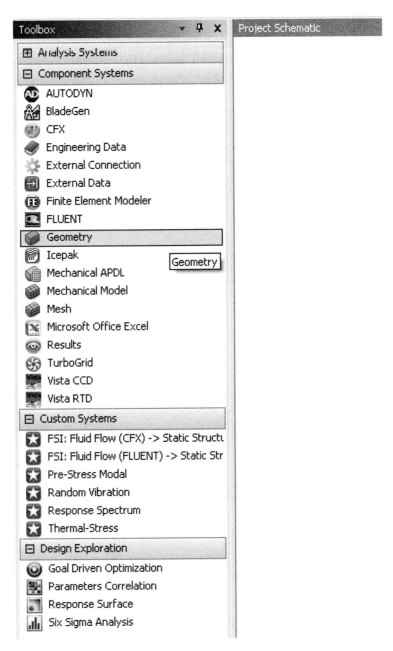

Figure I-4 Toolbox Component, Custom and Design Exploration options.

I-5 SUMMARY

The tutorials in this book explain some of the many engineering problem solution options available in ANSYS Workbench. It is important to remember that while practically anyone can learn which buttons to push to make the program work, the user must also give careful consideration to the assumptions inherent in the modeling process and perform an equally careful evaluation of the computed results.

In short, as you work through these tutorials keep in mind that model building and output evaluation based upon the sound fundamental **principles** of **engineering** and **physics** are the keys to using any program such as ANSYS Workbench correctly and successfully.

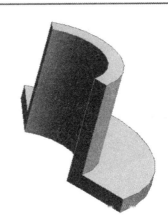

Chapter 1

Solid Modeling Fundamentals

1-1 OVERVIEW

A simple **L-shaped cross section** is used to introduce basic solid modeling concepts with ANSYS DesignModeler. These tutorials explore solid modeling by:

◆ Extruding

◆ Revolving

◆ Sweeping

A number of additional parametric, feature-based modeling possibilities and formulations are demonstrated in this chapter.

1-2 INTRODUCTION

Solid modeling can be accomplished in a number of ways, and one favorite method involves starting with a two-dimensional shape and manipulating it to create a solid. That is the approach we will use for many of the object models created in this book. Figure 1-1 shows an L-shaped cross section that has been variously **extruded, revolved,** or **swept along a curve** to produce the solid object models shown.

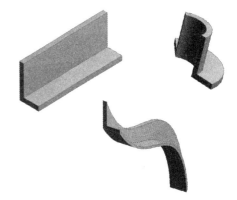

Figure 1-1 Extruding, revolving, sweeping an L-shaped section.

In the following we use this simple L-shaped section as well as a circular section to illustrate the three fundamental solid modeling approaches mentioned above.

1-3 TUTORIAL 1A – EXTRUSION

Follow the steps below to create a **solid model** of an **extrusion** with an **L-shaped** cross section.

1.   Follow the steps outlined in the previous chapter Figures I-1 through I-4 to **Start ANSYS Workbench. Double click Geometry** or **drag Geometry** into the **Project Schematic** as shown below.

Figure 1-2 Design Modeler in the Project Schematic.

The question mark indicates that **cell A-2** is incomplete.

2.   Select the **small blue triangle** for additional information

3. **Double click cell A-2 Geometry** to start **Design Modeler**. Select **millimeter** length units > **OK.**

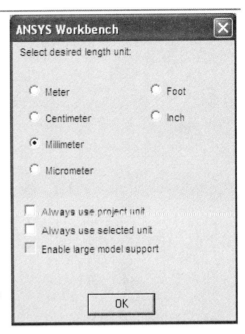

Figure 1-3 Work in millimeters.

We will **sketch** the L-shaped cross section on the XY Plane. Make it **35 mm high, 20 mm wide** with **5 mm thick legs**.

4. **Select XYPlane** as in the figure below. Then **click** on the **Look at icon** to view the XYPlane.

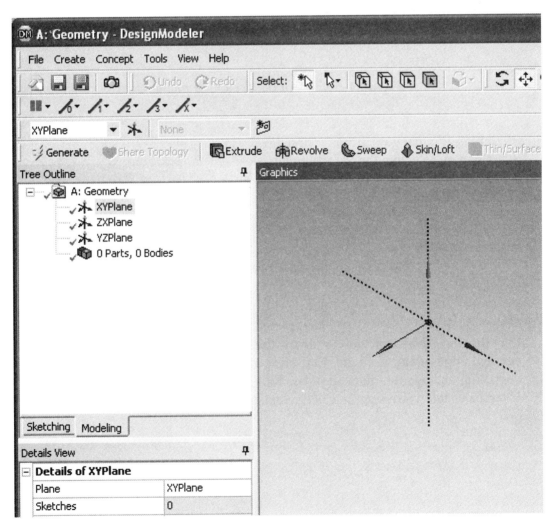

Figure 1-4 Select the sketching plane.

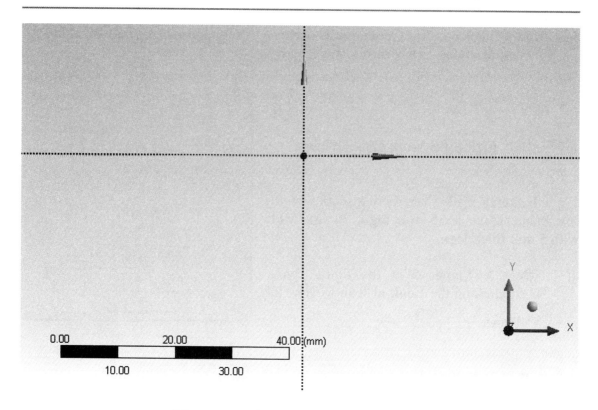

Figure 1-5 View of the sketching plane.

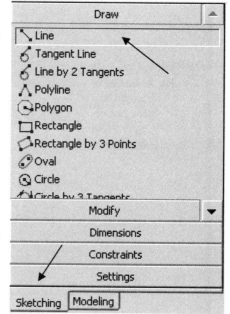

5.   Sketching. Change from Modeling to Sketching by selecting the Sketching tab.

Select **Draw > Line**

Figure 1-6 Sketching tools.

6.   Use the line drawing tool to draw the left vertical edge of the L-shape. Left click at the beginning and again at the end of the line. The **V** indicates that you've got it exactly **vertical**.

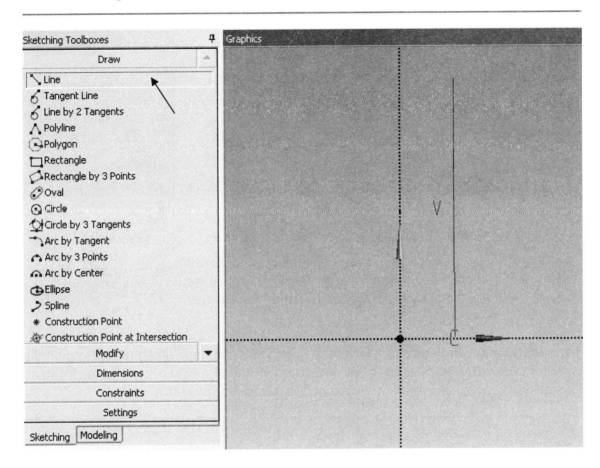

Figure 1-7 Left edge of the L-shape.

7. **Continue sketching** until you have something like what is shown below. Left click at the beginning and again at the end of each line. (Notice that the top edge is not quite horizontal.) If you need to change something, use **Undo** to back up or use **New Selection, Edge** filter to select a line, press the delete key and redraw it.   Also note that the cursor changes shape when it is **snapped** onto another point or axis.

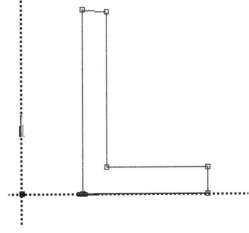

Figure 1-8 L-section sketch.

Use **constraint** options **horizontal** to make the top edge horizontal and **equal length** to make sure that the vertical and horizontal legs of the L are of the same thickness.

8. **Sketching > Constraints > Horizontal** –
    Left click the top edge.

Figure 1-9 Sketching constraints.

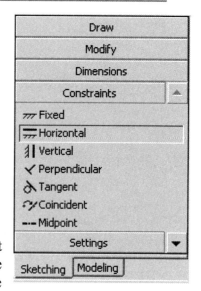

9.   **Sketching > Constraints > Equal length** –
      Left Click the top edge and then the right edge.

The figure is just a sketch so far, and a number of different dimensioning schemes could be used to produce the section we want. We will use the **Sketching > Dimensions** options to give it the desired properties.

10.   **Sketching > Dimensions > General** – Left click and (hold down the button) on the left vertical edge of the section and drag the dimension to a convenient location. The V1 means this is the first vertical dimension for this sketch.

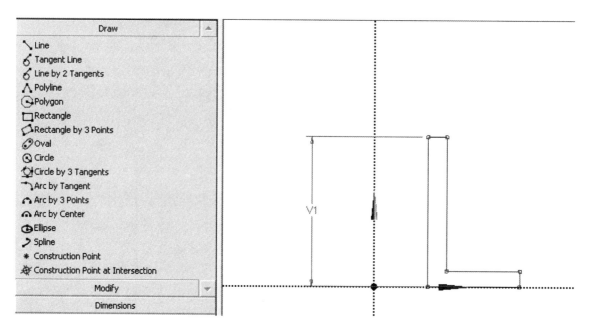

Figure 1-10 L-section sketch.

Continue with General dimensioning to specify H3 and V2. Don't dimension the top edge; it has to be equal to V2. The bottom edge is located directly on the X axis but we need to locate the vertical edge with respect to the Y axis.

11. **Sketching > Dimensions > Horizontal** – Left click the left vertical edge then click the dotted Y axis and drag the H3 dimension to a convenient location.

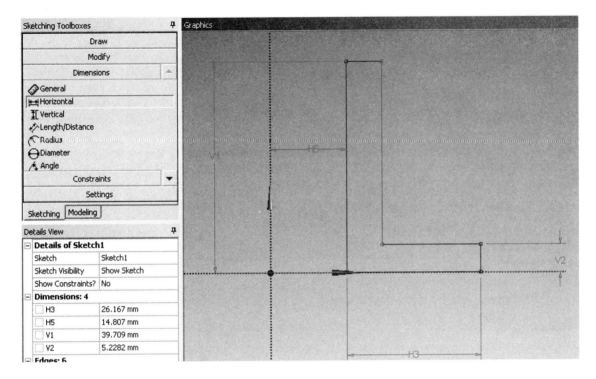

Figure 1-11 L-section sketch with all dimensions.

The current values for the dimensions depend upon the scale used in the sketching process, e.g., H3 = 21.126 mm in the **Details of Sketch1** box shown in figure above.

12. **Edit the dimensions to give them the desired values.** – Click on a value, enter the change and press return.

Figure 1-12 Default dimension values.

Details View	
□ **Details of Sketch1**	
Sketch	Sketch1
Sketch Visibility	Show Sketch
Show Constraints?	No
□ **Dimensions: 4**	
☐ H3	26.167 mm
☐ H5	14.807 mm
☐ V1	39.709 mm
☐ V2	5.2282 mm

13. **View > Ruler** (Top menu) to turn off the ruler display. Use the middle mouse roller to zoom in and out.

To reposition the section on the screen, **Right Click** in the graphics area of the display and select one of the following options: **Cursor Mode, View,** or **Zoom to Fit**.

The result is shown in the figure below.

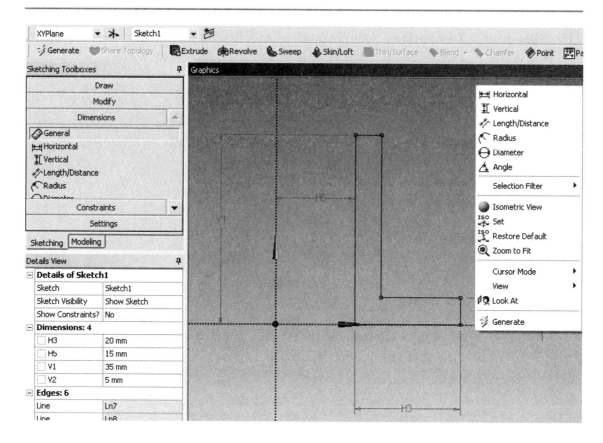

Figure 1-13 Edited dimension values.

To perform the extrusion, switch back from Sketching to Modeling. If it is not already highlighted, click **Sketch1** in the **Tree Outline** to highlight it.

14.   Modeling > Sketch1 > Extrude   [Extrude]

The L-shaped section will be extruded along the positive Z axis by the amount specified in the **Depth** field shown in the **Details of Extrude1** box (Figure 1-14). **Edit this value** to give the solid an extrude **depth** of **100 mm**.
The tree structure shows the components from which the solid model is created.

15.   Click the **Generate** icon to complete creation of the extruded shape model.

In the graphics area of the display **Right click > View > Isometric** (or hold down the middle mouse button and rotate the object).

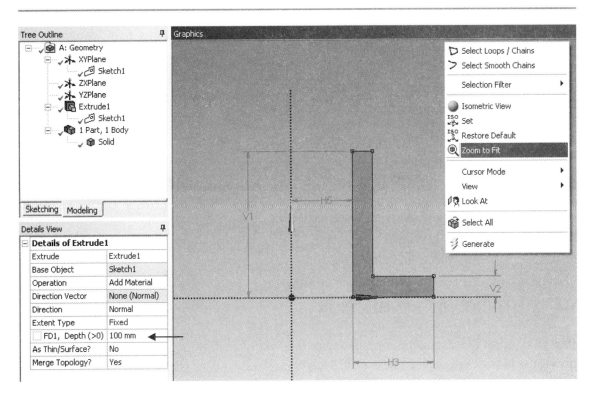

Figure 1-14 Extrusion.

16. **Click** on the **Display Plane** icon to turn off the axes display and high-light the last item in the model tree (Solid) to display the volume, surface area, faces, edges and vertices in this model.

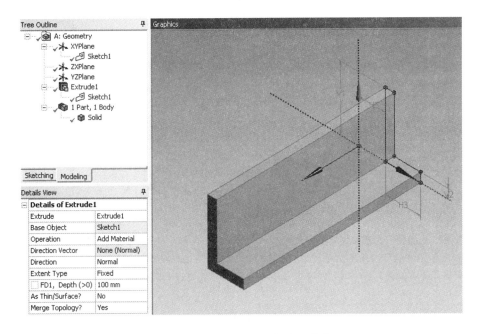

Figure 1-15 Extruded solid.

17. **Save your work** – Use the **Save As** option to save the extrusion using a name (e.g. T1A) and location of your choice.

Figure 1-16 File menu.

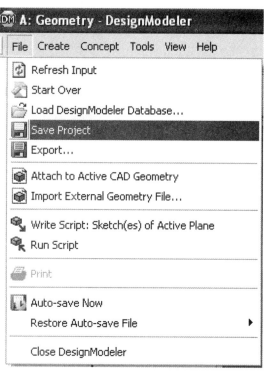

Basic solid modeling notions have been used thus far to demonstrate creating a solid by extruding a two-dimensional section. In the next tutorial we will revolve the same L-shape to create a solid of revolution.

1-4 TUTORIAL 1B – REVOLUTION

We can reuse the extrusion model from the previous tutorial after it has been safely saved. Start from the screen shown below if the extrusion is still in memory, or start Workbench and reload the extrusion. First modify the tree structure.

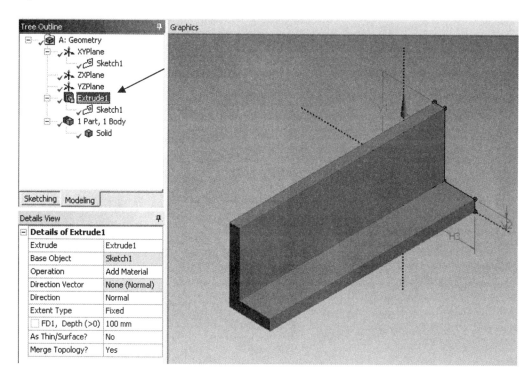

Figure 1-17 Select the extrusion.

1.   **Click on Extrude1** and **press Delete**. Click **Yes** to the query. The extrusion is deleted and the new tree structure shows 0 Parts and 0 Bodies.

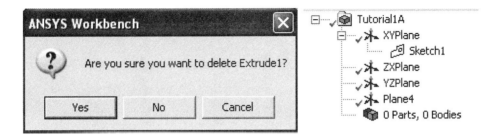

Figure 1-18 Delete the extrusion.

2.   Use **Save As** to save this work using a **new file name**, say **Tutorial1B**.

3.   **Click** on **Sketch1**, the **Display Plane** icon ✳ and the **Look at Plane** icon 🔍

We obtain the view of the same sketch we had earlier.

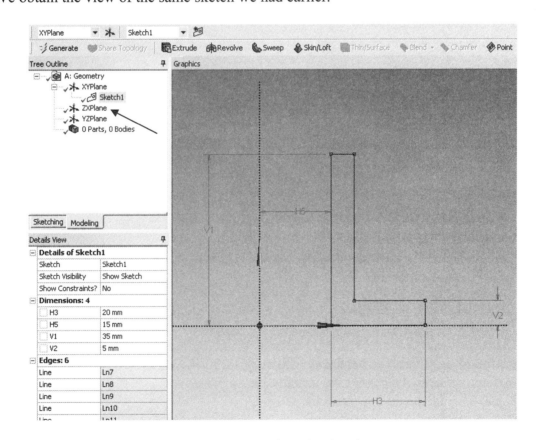

Figure 1-19 Select the sketch.

4.   Be sure **Sketch1 is highlighted** and **Click Revolve**.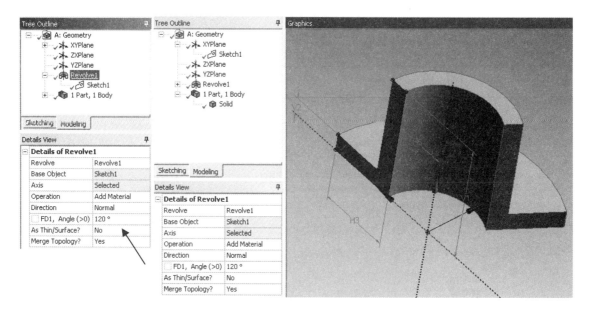

5.   **Click Axis > Select the Y axis > Apply** In **Details of Revolve1 box.**

6.   **Select Angle > Enter 120 deg**.

7.   **Click Generate.**

The L-shaped section is rotated about the Y axis by 120 degrees to create the solid of revolution shown next. **Direction** options change the rotation direction.

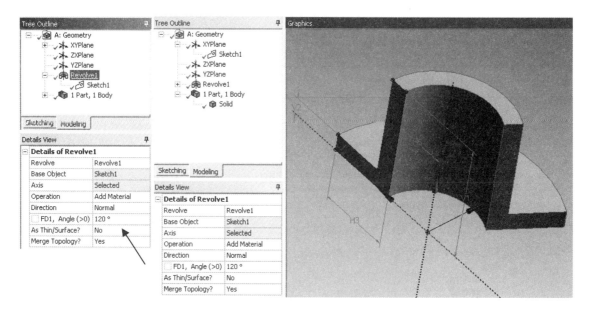

Figure 1-20 Solid of revolution.

8.   **Save** to archive your work.

Next we will take a **circular cross section** and **sweep it along** a **circular path** to illustrate the third kind of modeling discussed in this chapter.

1-5   TUTORIAL 1C – SWEEP

1.   **Start Design Modeler. Sketch a 2 mm diameter circle on the XYPlane** as before. We get the **sketch1** figure shown. Save this file as T1C or something convenient.

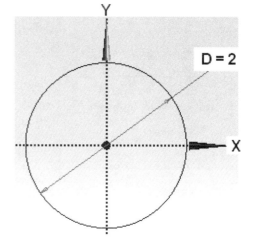

Figure 1-21 Cross section, **sketch1**.

We now want to sketch a path along which the circular shape will be swept to produce a solid. We will use a simple curve to define this path.

2. **Select the YZPlane** and **Select Sketching**.

3. Use the **Circle** and **Trim options** to sketch **a semi-circle of Radius 20 mm** in the **YZPlane** as shown below. Note that at the origin of the path, sketch2, is perpendicular to the cross section, sketch1.

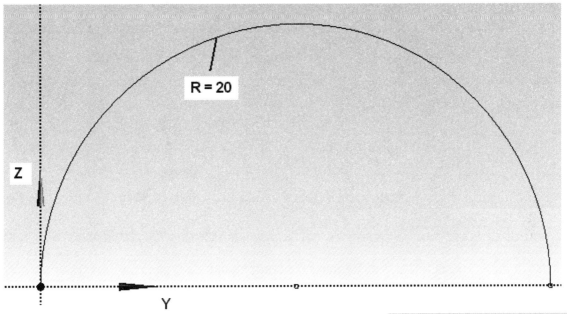

Figure 1-22 Path of sweep, **sketch2**.

4. **Select Sweep** to create the solid. Sweep

We need to specify the **Profile** (cross section) of the solid and the **Path** along which the profile will be swept.

5. In the Tree Outline Click **Sketch1**, then in **Details of Sweep1** > Click on **Profile** > **Apply**.

6. In the Tree Outline Click **Sketch2**, then in **Details of Sweep1** > **Path** > **Apply**

See the figure below.

⟶

Figure 1-23 Profile and path selection.

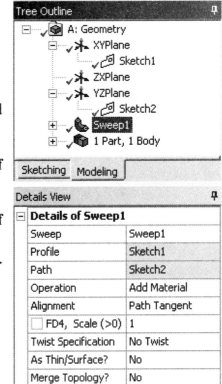

7.   **Generate** to obtain the solid shown next.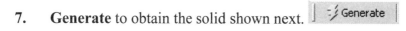

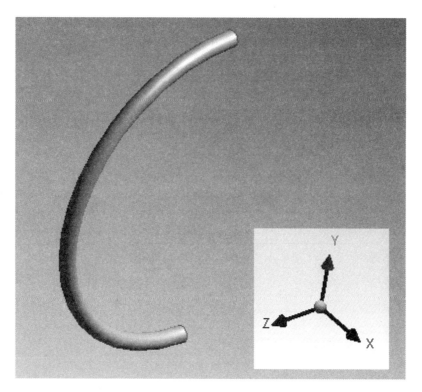

Figure 1-24 Swept solid.

Notice that the profile is perpendicular to the path as when we used Extrude to create a solid. Also the path can be a more complex curve as in the example of Figure 1-1 where a spline was used for the path.

1-6   SKETCHING

A wide variety of sketching tools are available to help in creating two-dimensional sections. We used the line drawing option and the equality constraint option in the tutorials above. Some of the other sketching features are shown below.

The next illustration shows the **Draw** and **Modify** options. The **Draw** menu includes **Line**, **Tangent Line**, **Line by two Tangents**, **Polyline**, **Polygon**, **Rectangle**, **Oval**, **Circle**, **Arc**, **Ellipse**, **Spline** and **Construction Point**.

The **Modify** menu includes **Fillet**, **Chamfer**, **Trim**, **Extend**, **Split**, **Drag**, **Cut**, **Copy**, **Paste**, **Move**, **Replicate** and **Offset**.

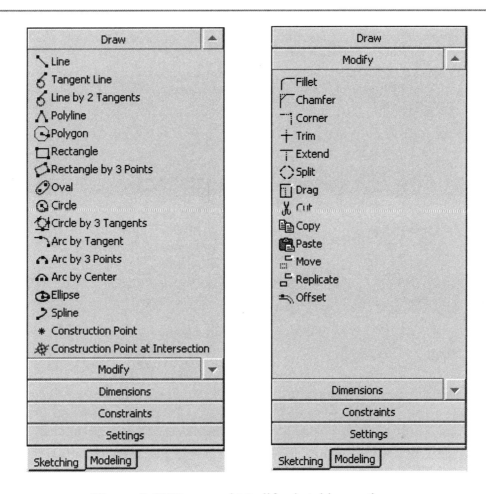

Figure 1-25 Draw and Modify sketching options.

We will have the occasion to illustrate the use of many of these options in what follows. Menu selections for assigning **Dimensions** and enforcing **Constraints** are shown in the next figure.

In addition to a **General** dimension specification, dimensions can be assigned which are **Horizontal, Vertical, Length/Distance, Radius/Diameter,** or an **Angle.** Select **Semi-Automatic Dimensioning** if you want DesignModeler to select a dimensioning scheme automatically. You then have the option to accept, add or delete dimensions to meet your specific design needs.

Constraints that can be enforced for sketching entities include **Horizontal, Vertical, Perpendicular, Tangent, Coincident, Midpoint, Symmetric, Parallel, Concentric, Equal Radius, Equal Length** and **Equal Distance**.

As sketching proceeds DesignModeler will attempt to detect and enforce constraints that seem to be part of the design intent of the sketch. The **Auto Constraints** option allows you to turn these on and off as desired. **Cursor** triggered constraints are local, while **Global** constraints relate to all entities in the sketching plane.

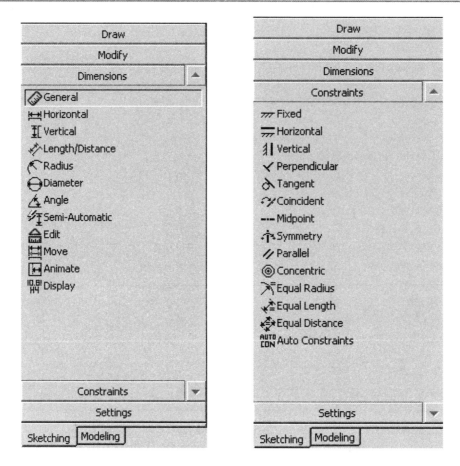

Figure 1-26 Dimension and Constraint sketching options.

Dimensioning is the process of defining how geometry is to be constructed.

In that regard, sketches must be **unambiguously** defined; that is, they cannot have too many dimensions or too few dimensions specified. The figure below shows two different dimensioning schemes for a simple shape.

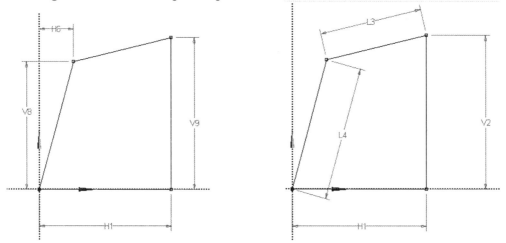

Figure 1-27 Two different dimensioning schemes.

If you over-dimension a sketch, DesignModeler will issue the following warning:

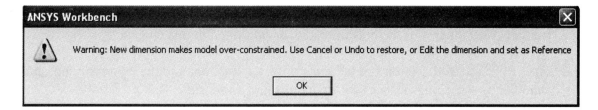

Figure 1-28 Over-constraint message.

Finally, the **Settings** option provides a **grid** sketching aid that allows you create drawing entities placed at vertices of the grid as indicated in the next figure.

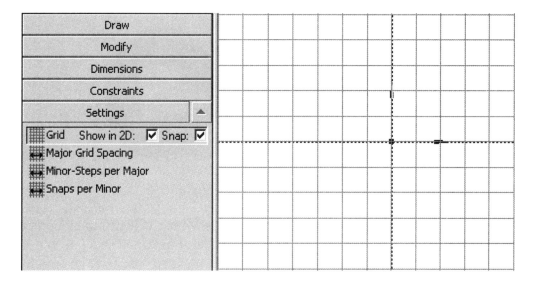

Figure 1-29 Settings options and a sketching grid.

1-7 SUMMARY

Three tutorials in Chapter 1 introduce basic solid model creation in ANSYS DesignModeler and provide examples from which more complex shapes can be developed. In the next chapter we will extend these ideas and introduce additional modeling features.

1-8   PROBLEMS

1-1   Identify some common objects (such as an unsharpened pencil, drinking glass, etc.) and develop models of them using the ideas presented in this chapter.

1-2   Use a "T" shaped section to create a solid by extrusion, another by revolving, and another by sweeping. Select your own units and dimensions.

1-3   Measure the exterior dimensions of a light bulb, estimate the wall thickness of the glass and base, and create a model by revolving the sketch.

1-4   Create the shape shown and extrude it to form a solid. Choose your own dimensions. Use the Sketching **Trim** option to help in the sketch development. Save it and we'll use it in a simulation problem later in the text.

Figure P1-4   **Figure P1-5**

1-5   A 20 inch diameter cylinder has an 8 in square hole with 1.0 inch radius corner fillets. The thickness is 0.75 inch. Create the solid model shown.

1-6   Create the solid model shown below.

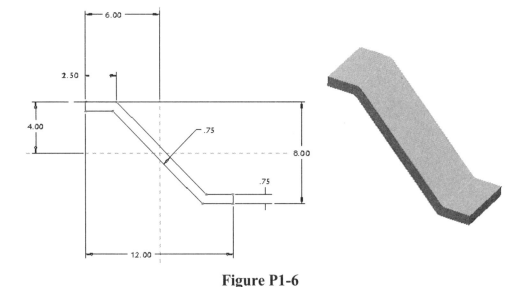

Figure P1-6

1-7   The cross section of the upper half of a flat-topped cylinder is shown below. The
dimensions are in millimeters. Create a solid model of the cylinder.

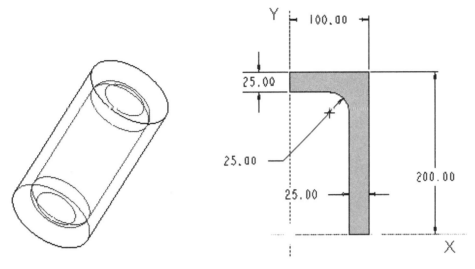

Figure P1-7

NOTES:

Chapter 2

Placed Features, Assembly

2-1 OVERVIEW

In this chapter we illustrate DesignModeler creation of features whose **shape** is **predetermined**. Among these are

- ♦ Holes

- ♦ Rounds

- ♦ Chamfers

- ♦ Patterns

In addition to these topics, at the end of the chapter we illustrate simple **assembly modeling** in ANSYS DesignModeler.

2-2 INTRODUCTION

Feature-based solid modeling involves the creation of part models by combining various features. The features illustrated in Chapter 1 are sometimes called **sketched features** because they were based upon sketched cross sections we created. Sketched features can have virtually any shape we desire. The basic parts of Chapter 1 can also be called **base features** since we started from scratch each time and created a new part.

We can add features to base features to create more complex parts. If these added features have predetermined shapes they are often called **placed features** because all we need to do is specify the location or placement of the new feature on an existing base feature.

The figure below shows the L-shaped Extrusion created earlier with a **hole**, a **round** and a **chamfer** added to it. This demonstrates the manner in which features can be added to a base feature in order to create more complicated and useful parts with the shapes desired for specific tasks.

The tutorials that follow illustrate how to add these placed features to the basic parts created in Chapter 1.

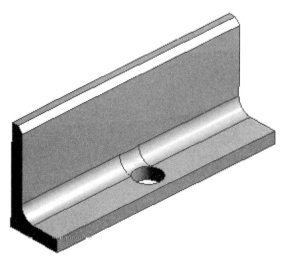

Figure 2-1 Extrusion with placed features.

2-3   TUTORIAL 2A – ADDING A HOLE TO THE EXTRUSION

Follow the steps below to cut a hole in the top face of the short leg of the Chapter 1 extrusion.

Start ANSYS Workbench and reload the L-section Extrusion

1.   **ANSYS > Workbench > DesignModeler Geometry > Browse > Tutorial1A** (or the file name you chose)

Now save this file under a new name for this tutorial

2.   **File > Save As > Tutorial2A** (or another name you select)

We want to create the hole on the top surface of the short leg of the extrusion. We will create a new plane on which to place the circle that generates the hole.

3.   **Selection Filter: Model Faces (3D)**

4.   **Click on the top surface of the short leg.**

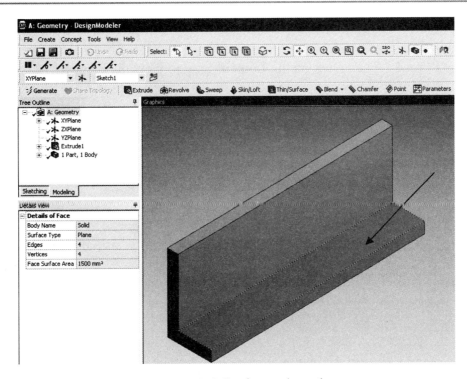

Figure 2-2 Surface selected.

5.   Create > New Plane (from the top menu)

A new plane is added to the tree structure (Plane4 in this illustration; your plane number may be different) and an axis system is provided.

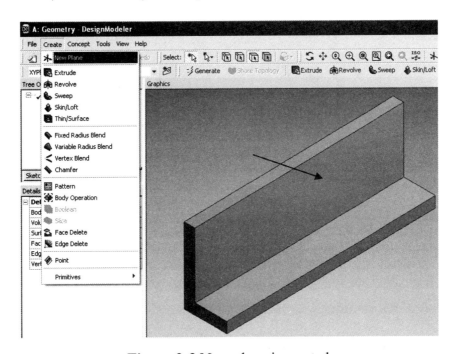

Figure 2-3 New plane is created.

6.   Click Generate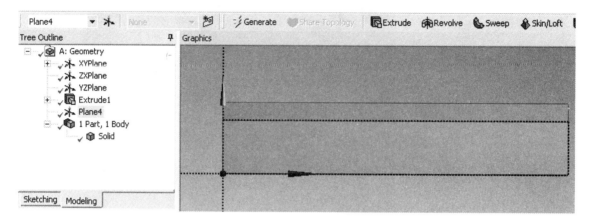

7.   Select Plane4 > Then **click** on the **Look at icon** to view the Plane4

Figure 2-4 'Look at' new plane.

We want to place a **10 mm diameter** circular hole **half way** along the length of the 100 mm leg and **8 mm** from the edge.

8.   Sketching > Circle Draw a circle on the top face as shown in the figure below.

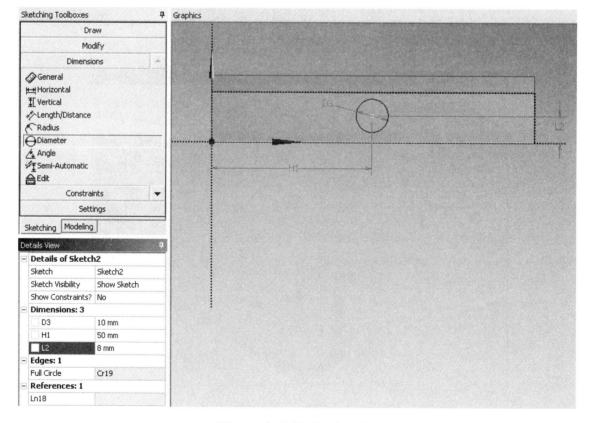

Figure 2-5 Circle sketch.

9.   **Dimensions > Diameter** – Place D3 as shown.

10. **Dimensions > Horizontal** – Place H1 as shown.

11. **Dimensions > Length** – Place L2 as shown.

Edit the dimension values to 10 mm, 50 mm, and 8 mm as shown in the figure above. (The number attached to each dimension, the 2 in H1, is an internal numbering scheme and depends upon the sketching sequence. Your numbers may be different.)

12. **Modeling > Click** on **Sketch** in the tree structure (Sketch2 in the figure)

13. **Extrude**   Extrude

14. **Operation > Cut Material**

(Remove material instead of adding it.)

15. **Type > Through All**

(Cut completely through the thickness, through all.)

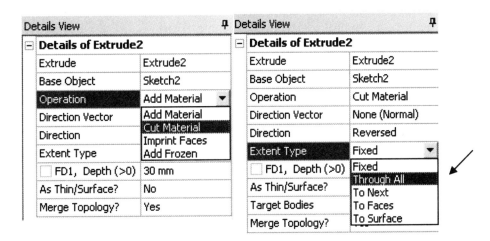

Figure 2-6 Extrude details.

16. **Generate** (to complete the feature.)   Generate

The completed hole is shown in the next illustration.

Figure 2-7 Circular hole.

Keep this part in memory since we have more work to do on it.

2-4   TUTORIAL 2B – ADDING A ROUND TO THE EXTRUSION

A gradual transition between surfaces is variously called a **fillet**, a **round** or a **blend**.
DesignModeler uses the blend terminology, and a blend
is a placed feature. In this tutorial we will place a fixed
radius blend at the inside corner of the L where the top
surface of the short leg meets the inside vertical surface.

Save your part using a new name.

1.   File > Save As > Tutorial2B

Set the selection filter.

2.   Selection Filter: Edges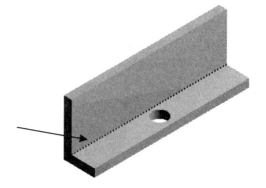

3.   Select the inside edge of the part.

Figure 2-8 Select the edge.

4.   Create > Fixed Radius Blend

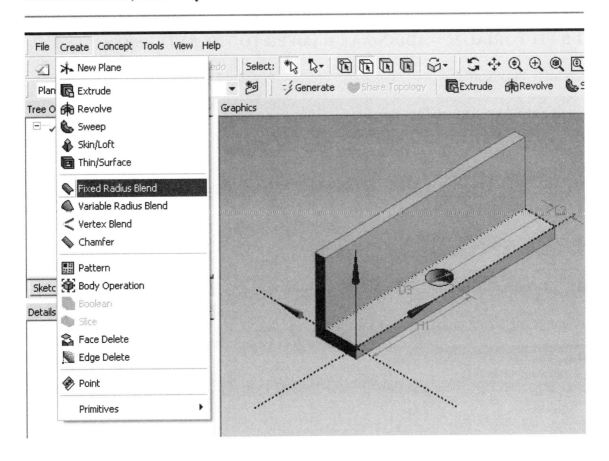

Figure 2-9 Selecting the blend option.

5.   Geometry > Apply

(Use the default 3 mm radius.)   **Generate**

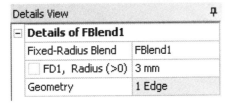

Figure 2-10 The blend completed.

2-5   TUTORIAL 2C – ADDING A CHAMFER TO THE EXTRUSION

Creating the chamfer is pretty much like creating the blend.

1.   **Save As > Tutorial2C**
      (Save the part under a new name if you wish)

2.   **Selection Filter: Edges**

3.   **Select the top inside edge of the part**.

4.   **Create > Chamfer**

5.   **Details of Chamfer > Geometry > Apply**

(Change the sizing to 2.5 mm.)

Figure 2-11 Select chamfer.

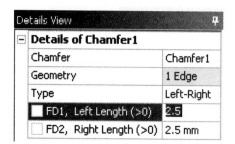

6.   **Generate**

7.   **Save your work**

Figure 2-12 The chamfer completed.

2-6 TUTORIAL 2D – PATTERNS

Next we will use a **pattern operation** to create a solid model of circular plate with a symmetric bolt pattern. First extrude a circle to create a **50 mm diameter** plate that is **10 mm** in **thickness** as shown in the next figure. Start a new part file.

1. **Sketch a 50 mm diameter circle** with center at the origin of the **XYPlane**. Click on the sketch then on **Extrude** and set the extrusion depth to be **10 mm**. Click Generate to complete the base feature disk.

2. **Sketching > Dimensions > Display >** check both **Name** and **Value**.

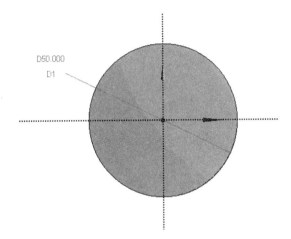

Figure 2-13 Base feature disk.

3. **Create > New Plane** Create a new plane for sketching on the **top or bottom surface** of the base disk

4. **Sketch an 8mm diameter circle** on this plane. Dimension as shown in the next figure.

5. **Sketch an 18 mm line** from the **center of the base feature** to the **center of the small circle**. Dimension as shown below. We'll use this line for angular reference.

6. **Locate the line with an angular dimension.** Click first on the horizontal axis, then on the line. Drag to place the dimension as shown.

7. **Switch to Modeling. Select the sketch and then Extrude > Cut Material > Through All** to create a hole.

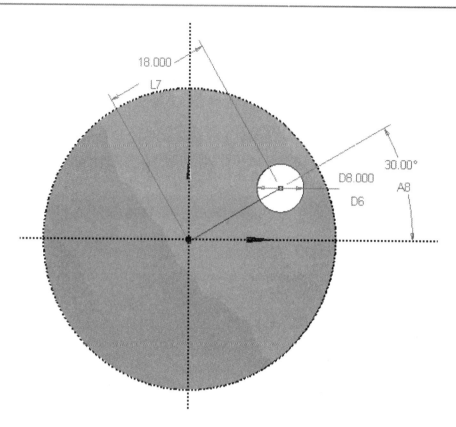

Figure 2-14 Placement of small hole.

8.   **Add a 1 mm chamfer to the top edge of the 8 mm hole.** See figure next page.

9.   **Sketch a short line along the Z axis** in the ZXPlane. Sketch3. We will use this for the pattern angular direction reference later.

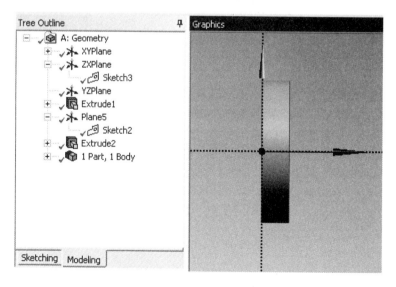

Figure 2-15 Create a line along the Z axis.

10.   **Click Selection Filter: Model Faces (3D)**

11.   **Select the inside surface of the hole**; then **Ctrl > Select** the **surface** of the **chamfer** so both items will be in the pattern.

Figure 2-16 Select the chamfer and hole.

12.   **Create > Pattern**

13.   **Geometry > Apply** (in details of Pattern1.)

14.   **Pattern Type > Circular**

15.   **Selection Filter: Edges**

16.   **Axis > Click on Sketch3** and select the **short Z axis line > Apply**

17.   **Angle > Evenly Spaced**

18.   **Number of Copies > 6** (Creates 7 instances total.)

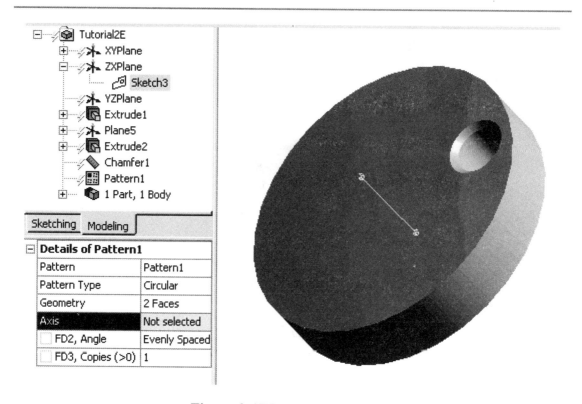

Figure 2-17 Pattern parameters.

19.   Click Generate   ⚡ Generate

The resulting hole pattern is shown next. The **selected edge** is used as the **axis** for determining the positive direction of incrementing the angular placement (taken according to the right-hand rule).

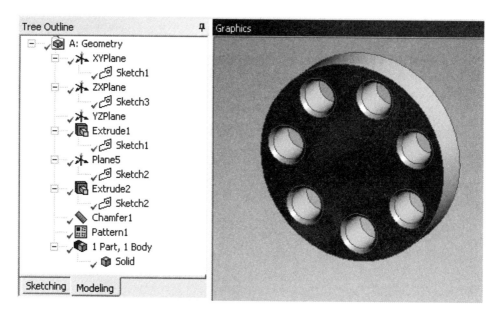

Figure 2-18 Circular pattern of chamfered holes.

Once again don't be surprised if the suffix numbers of the entities (Sketch, Extrude, etc) in your tree structures differ from those in the figures. Same with the lighting bolts indicating need for generation. Some experimentation with generation, views, etc. was conducted to obtain the figures presented here. If you have a problem, delete the problem object in the tree and start again.

(The positive direction for incrementing the angular placement is along the selected edge according to the right-hand rule. **Change Evenly Spaced to 35 degrees > 6 Copies** and see what solid is produced.)

Linear patterns are created using similar steps. The direction of the pattern can be along an existing edge or perpendicular to a surface.

2-7   TUTORIAL 2E – CLEVIS ASSEMBLY

The next figure shows an assembly model of the clevis device that is the subject of this final tutorial in this chapter.

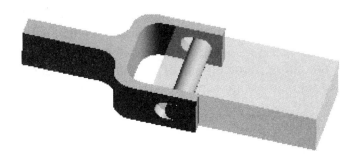

Figure 2-19 Clevis assembly.

1.   **Start DesignModeler, Select Inches Units, and start sketching on the XYPlane**

The yoke is 4.5 inches in overall length, 2.5 inches at its widest point, and the opening is 2.0 inches in width. Use the sketching tools to create the figure shown next with dimensions as indicated. **Arc by Tangent, Modify > Trim**, and other tools will come in handy. If you make a mistake, just delete the item in question and redraw, or just start over.

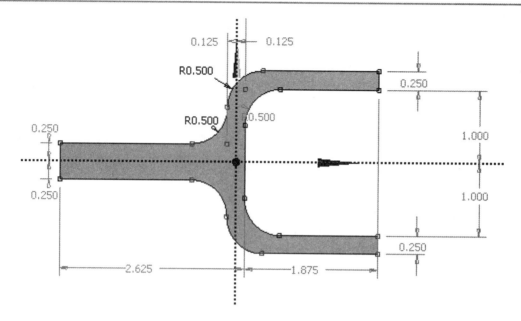

Figure 2-20 Clevis sketch.

2. **Create the sketch** shown above and **extrude it symmetrically 0.5 inch**. (Total height will be 1.0 inch, 0.5 above the sketch plane, 0.5 inch below.)

3. **Create a new sketching plane** on one of the yoke fingers and **sketch the opening** shown. The two semicircles are separated by 0.25 inch. Tangent line and trim will be useful.

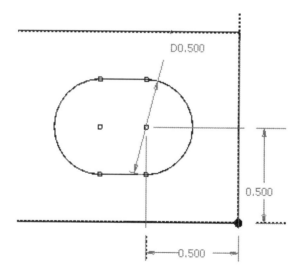

Figure 2-21 Slot sketch.

4. **Extrude this sketch through all, removing material.**

We obtain the solid model shown next.

Figure 2-22 Complete clevis.

To this we want to add the stem and pin to complete the assembly. First **hide the clevis**.

5.   **1 Parts, 1 Body > Solid > Right Click > Hide Body**

6.   We'll create the **stem** first. **View the XZ sketch plane** and **sketch the rectangle and circle** below for creation of the **brick-shaped stem extrusion.** Use **General** for the linear dimension definitions.

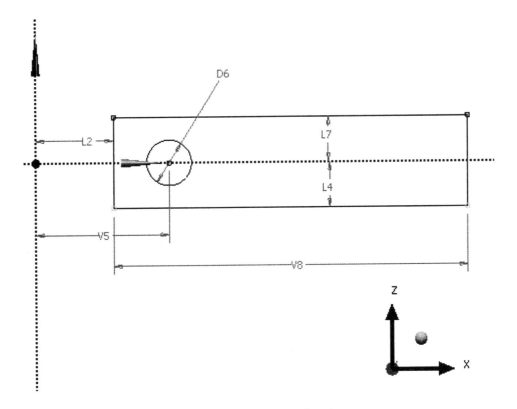

Figure 2-23 Stem sketch.

Refer to Figure 2-20 and give the L2 and V5 placements dimensions the values shown below.

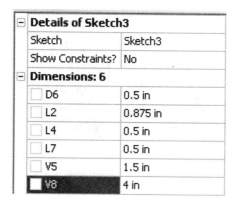

Details of Sketch3	
Sketch	Sketch3
Show Constraints?	No
Dimensions: 6	
D6	0.5 in
L2	0.875 in
L4	0.5 in
L7	0.5 in
V5	1.5 in
V8	4 in

Figure 2-24 Stem sketch dimensions.

7.   **Switch to Modeling, Select the sketch** of the **Rectangle** with **Circle**, Click **Extrude**.

8.   **Details of Extrude > Operation > Add Frozen, Direction > Both – Symmetric**, and **Depth > 1.0** (See below.)

The **Add Frozen** option adds the stem as a new, separate object and does not merge the new geometry into the existing clevis. The two parts remain separate.

9.   **Generate** Generate

10.   **2 Parts, 2 Bodies > Solid** (Clevis) **> Right Click > Show Body**

Details of Extrude10	
Extrude	Extrude10
Base Object	Sketch3
Operation	Add Frozen
Direction Vector	None (Normal)
Direction	Both - Symmetric
Type	Fixed
FD1, Depth (>0)	1 in
As Thin/Surface?	No
Merge Topology?	Yes

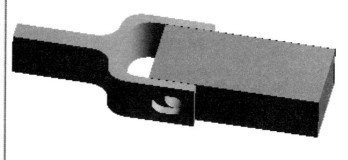

Figure 2-25 Stem extrusion and clevis.

Lastly we need to create the fastening pin that holds the assembly together. Create a new plane to sketch on.

11. **Click XZ Plane > Click** the **new plane icon** 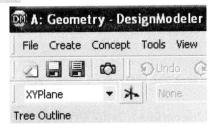 on the third line of icons > **Generate**

Figure 2-26 New plane icon.

12. **Right click on graphics screen > View > Bottom** to get the view shown below.

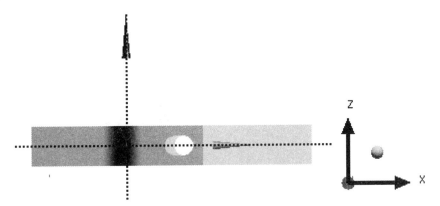

Figure 2-27 View for sketching pin.

13. **Sketch > Circle**

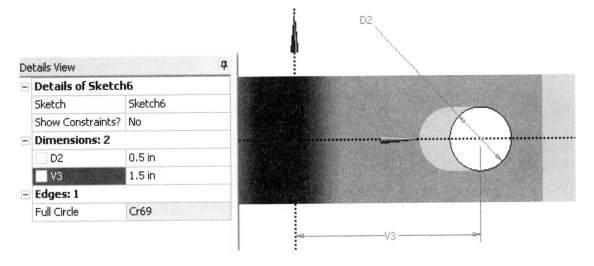

Figure 2-28 Pin sketch.

Put the center of the circle on the X Axis; Dimension its diameter and location from the Z Axis. Set the diameter to **0.5 inches** and the horizontal distance from the Z Axis to **1.5 inches**. (See Figure 2-20.)

Now create the pin extrusion using this sketch.

14.   **Switch to Modeling, Select the sketch** of the **Circle,** Click **Extrude.**

15.   **Details of Extrude > Operation > Add Frozen; Direction > Both – Symmetric; Depth > 1.25**

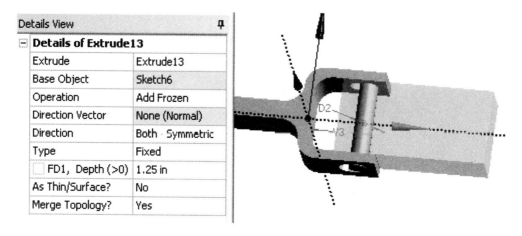

Figure 2-29 Final clevis, stem, pin assembly.

At any time use the middle mouse button to rotate the view so you can see the sketch plane with respect to the rest of the model and turn the axis and dimensions on/off by clicking the icon on the second row.

16.   **Save your work.** We'll use an assembly such as this later.

2-8   TUTORIAL 2F – ALTERNATE SOLID MODELER

Finally we outline the steps to utilize an alternate solid modeler (Pro/E, CATIA, etc.) for the creation of the clevis assembly.

1.   **Start the alternate solid modeler and create the clevis, stem, and pin parts.**

You can start over completely in the alternate solid modeler or you can save one or more of the parts from Tutorial 2E in the **STEP** or the **IGES** neutral file format and import them into the alternate solid modeler. (To extract an individual part from the model created above, delete the unwanted objects from the model tree and save the remaining desired object with a new name.)

Figure 2-30 Neutral file transfer.

2. Create the Assembly in the Alternate solid modeler.

With the alternate solid modeler running and the assembly you created in the alternate modeler as the active session in that modeler, (Windows systems):

3. Start ANSYS DesignModeler

4. File > ▣ Attach to Active CAD Geometry > Generate ⟨ ⌇ Generate⟩

The next figure shows the clevis assembly as created in Pro/ENGINEER. In DesignModeler the stem and the pin parts were deleted and the clevis was saved as a file in the IGES format (Sometimes STEP is better.). The clevis IGES file was then imported into Pro/E and saved as a Pro/E 'prt' file. The stem and pin parts were created in Pro/E, and the assembly was created in Pro/E and opened as the active session in Pro/E. Finally the Pro/E assembly was attached in DesignModeler using steps 3 and 4 above.

Figure 2-31 Assembly attached from an active Pro/E session.

Another approach is to save the assembly in the alternate solid modeler as an IGES or STEP file then to import the IGES or STEP assembly file into DesignModeler.

IGES (**I**nitial **G**raphics **E**xchange **S**pecification) and STEP (**St**andard for the **E**xchange of **P**roduct Model Data) are industry agreed upon neutral file formats for the exchange of modeling information.

During installation of ANSYS Workbench, be sure to install the geometry interfaces to the alternate solid modelers you are using. For Pro/E, for example, it is necessary to indicate the path to the Pro/E executable.

2-9 SUMMARY

The three tutorials in Chapter 2 illustrate basic placed feature creation and simple assembly modeling in ANSYS DesignModeler. In the next chapter we will extend these ideas to more complex parts and introduce additional solid modeling options.

2-10   PROBLEMS

2-1   Use the ideas presented above to add holes, blends and chamfers to the parts you created as end-of-chapter problems for Chapter 1.

2-2   Create a linear pattern of holes in a straight line on a rectangular plate of your design.

2-3   Use the holes in the exercise above to create a multiple hole pattern in the other direction of the plate.

Figure P2-2   **Figure P2-3**

2-4   Create a solid model of the object shown using the dimensions in Chapter 5.

2-5   Place a hole as shown below in the part created in Chapter 1.

2-6   Create a solid model of the object shown using the dimensions in Chapter 8.

Figure P2-4   **Figure P2-5**   **Figure P2-6**

NOTES:

Chapter 3

Modeling Techniques

3-1 OVERVIEW

This Chapter discusses modeling techniques that illustrate the flexibility inherent in the feature-based parametric modeling of DesignModeler. We consider the use of

♦ Parameters

♦ Other CAD systems

♦ Surface and line models

3-2 INTRODUCTION

The defining dimensions in the sketches, extrusions, revolves, sweeps, and placed features discussed in the previous Chapters were described using fixed numerical values according to the situation. In **parametric design modeling** we wish to assign **parameters** to these quantities so that they can be varied to fit various design requirements. It is also possible to write equations that relate the required variation in certain parameters in terms of other parameters. For example, it might be important for a hole always to be centered in a bracket even if different designs require that the bracket width change with application. Tutorial 3A illustrates this use of parameters.

DesignModeler is a full-featured parametric design modeling system that provides for importation of models from other CAD systems and also allows the user to export models to other CAD systems. One vehicle for doing this is the use of the standard neutral file formats IGES (**I**nitial **G**raphics **E**xchange **S**pecification) and STEP (**St**andard for the **E**xchange of **P**roduct Model Data), agreed upon standards for the transfer of models between systems.

Parts in DesignModeler are composed of **Bodies** whereas **Assemblies** may be composed of **Parts**. We illustrate these concepts also in this Chapter.

3-3 TUTORIAL 3A – PARAMETERS

The steps below illustrate the use of **parameters** and **parametric equations** to define relationships required for the execution of a particular design. The part in question is shown in the figure below. Here we wish the long leg of the bracket always to be 1.5 times the length of the short leg. The bracket thickness is to be constant. These invariant design requirements are accomplished using parametric relations in DesignModeler.

1. **Start ANSYS Workbench** and use **polyline** to **sketch on the XYPlane an L-section 25 mm x 15 mm x 2 mm thick. Sketching > Dimensions > Display** check **Name** and **Value**.

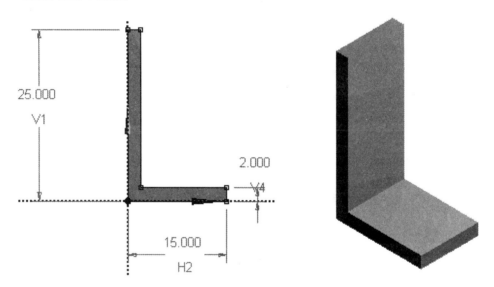

Figure 3-1 Bracket.

2. **Select the sketch** and **Extrude it 10 mm** (Save a copy of this model for use later.)

Details of Sketch1	
Sketch	Sketch1
Sketch Visibility	Show Sketch
Show Constraints?	No
Dimensions: 3	
H2	15 mm
V1	25 mm
V3	2 mm

Details of Extrude1	
Extrude	Extrude1
Base Object	Sketch1
Operation	Add Material
Direction Vector	None (Normal)
Direction	Normal
Type	Fixed
FD1, Depth (>0)	10 mm
As Thin/Surface?	No
Merge Topology?	Yes

Figure 3-2 Sketch and extrusion details.

The figure above shows the details of the sketch and extrusion. The sketch and extrude details boxes give us manual control over the size of the part. Edit any one of the dimensions shown in these detail boxes then click **Generate**, and you see the part size change immediately.

However in this exercise we want to access the dimensions used for this part and turn some of them into parameters that will provide greater control over the part dimensions and the interrelation between them.

3.   **First click on Sketch1** in the tree outline to bring up the details window then **Click the check box** just to the left of the dimension **V1** in the **Details of Sketch1**. (Your numbers may be different.)

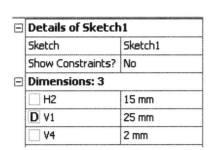 

Figure 3-3 Dialog box for parameter XYPlane.V1.

XYPlane.V1 is the dimension of the long leg of the bracket. Notice the D automatically placed in the check box to indicate that this quantity is '**Driven**' by **parameters** and **parameter relations**. It is usually most useful if the parameters are given names meaningful to the part. The XYPlane.V1 parameter will be named '**LongLeg**'. (XYPlane.H2 will be named '**ShortLeg**' and Extrude1.FD1 will be named '**BracketWidth**'.)

Enter **LongLeg** in the **Parameter Name box** and **Click OK**.

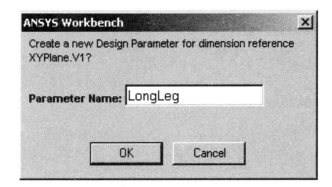

Figure 3-4 XYPlane1.V1 parameter.

Do the same for XYPlane.H2 and enter the name **ShortLeg**.

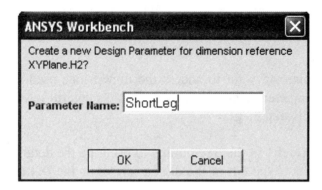

Figure 3-5 Dialog box for parameter XYPlane.H2, ShortLeg.

We will leave the check box for V4 alone since the thickness V4 is to remain constant at 2 mm.

4.   **Select Extrude1** and **Click the check box** just to the left of the dimension **FD1** in the **Details of Extrude1**. Accept this Design Parameter; **Click OK**.

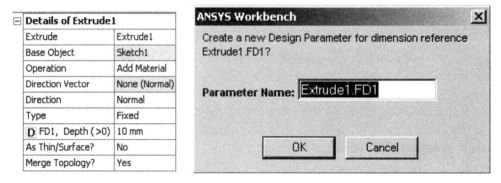

Figure 3-6 Dialog box for parameter Extrude1.FD1.

Extrude1.FD1 is the **parameter** for the length of the extrusion. Enter **BracketWidth** in the Parameter Name box and **Click OK**.

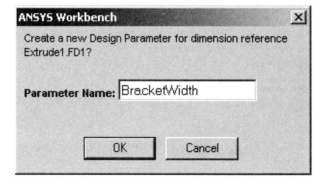

Figure 3-7 Extrude1.FD1 parameter.

We now have defined all of the parameters we want for the bracket dimensions. To view these, click the **Parameters icon** 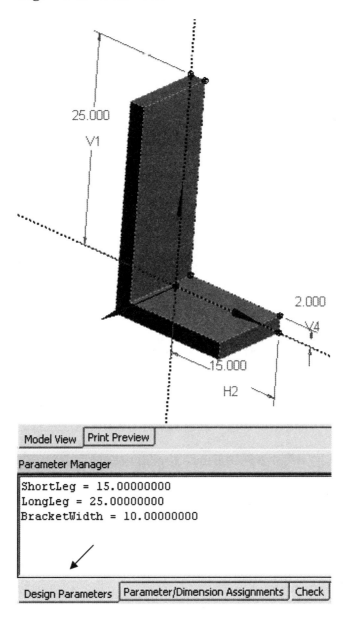, or use the **tools menu**.

5. Tools > Parameters

The parameters we have defined and their values are now shown at the **bottom of the screen** under the **Design Parameters Tab**.

Figure 3-8 Initial dimensions.

6. Click the **Parameter/Dimension Assignments Tab**

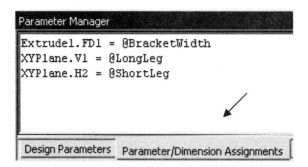

Figure 3-9 Parameter/Dimension Assignments tab.

The Parameter/Dimension Assignments window displays equation assignments used to drive the model dimensions. The design parameters are given an "@" prefix.

We can edit information in this window and add to these definitions in order to impose the relations between dimensions that we desire. Comments are preceded by the "#" character.

In the example under consideration we want the XYPlane.V1 dimension to be 1.5 times the ShortLeg dimension and the other values as defined. Enter these relations in the Parameter/Dimension Assignments window as shown below.

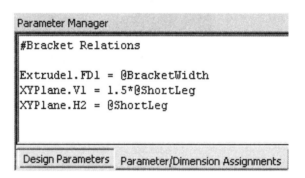

Figure 3-10 Bracket relation equations.

Then press **Generate** to create the bracket with new size variables as shown in the figure below.

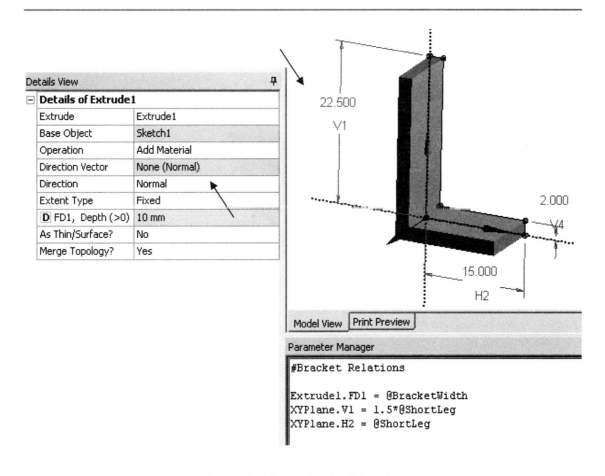

Figure 3-11 Newly sized bracket.

Notice that the H2 dimension remains at 15 mm and the height (long leg) is adjusted to 22.5 mm. These relations persist and are enforced for any subsequent changes we make to ShortLeg. For example, Click on the Design Parameters Tab to edit the values shown. If we change the **ShortLeg** to **5 mm** and click **Generate**, we get the part shown next.

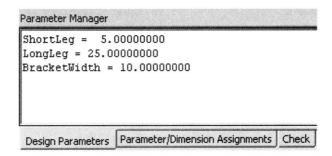

Figure 3-12 Edit dimension values.

The H2/V1 proportions will change according to the relations assigned, but the bracket thickness will remain 2 mm.

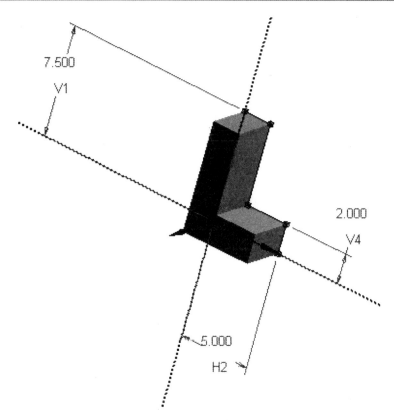

Figure 3-13 Newly sized bracket.

7.   Click the **Parameter/Dimension Assignments Tab**

The Check Tab is used to check the syntax of the relations you have entered. For example if @LongLeg appears on the left of an assignment equation, a syntax error will be created, and the part will not be generated correctly.

```
Parameter Manager

### DesignModeler Parameter/Dimension Assignments Output
 1 | Comment     |            | #Bracket Relations
 2 | Comment     |            |
 3 | Feature Dim | 10.0000 | Extrude1.FD1 = @BracketWidth
 4 | Plane Dim   |  7.5000 | XYPlane.V1 = 1.5*@ShortLeg
 5 | Plane Dim   |  5.0000 | XYPlane.H2 = @ShortLeg

### DesignModeler Design Parameter Assignments Output
 1 |             |  5.0000 | @ShortLeg                    |
 2 |             | 25.0000 | @LongLeg                     |
 3 |             | 10.0000 | @BracketWidth                |

 Design Parameters | Parameter/Dimension Assignments | Check | Close
```

Figure 3-14 Check Tab.

8.   Change back to the original dimensions when you are finished and **Click Parameter Manager** to **Close** the window. **Save T3A**.

Design parameters appear as the CAD parameters in **Analysis Modules** if their names contain the **Parameter Key** defined when starting the analysis. The **default parameter key** is **DS**. If all design parameters are to be sent to the associated analysis, make the parameter key blank when you start the simulation.

3-4 OTHER CAD SYSTEMS

DesignModeler provides support for a number of other widely used CAD systems. When using Windows-based systems, you can bring a model currently being edited in a CAD session on your computer (Pro/E, CATIA, etc.) into DesignModeler by using

File > Attach to Active CAD Geometry

The model then appears as an object in the feature tree of your DesignModeler session.

Alternate CAD system geometry interface support includes **Autodesk Inventor, Autodesk Mechanical Desktop, CATIA, Pro/ENGINEER, Solid Edge, SolidWorks**, and **Unigraphics**.

The **IGES** and **STEP** neutral file exchange formats for 2D or 3D CAD product models, drawings, or graphics is also supported by DesignModeler. (See also Chapter 2) The bracket model shown here was created in Pro/ENGINEER, saved in the IGES format, then imported in DesignModeler using

File > Import External Geometry File > bracket.igs > Generate

Figure 3-15 IGES import.

Models created in DesignModeler can also be **exported** in the IGES or **STEP** format for use with other CAD, graphics, or analysis software. Use the following sequence to export the file in the current DesignModeler session.

File > Export > IGES (*.igs, *.iges)   (or **STEP**)

3-5 SURFACE AND LINE MODELS

Surface models are necessary if one wishes to perform analysis using simplified planar or 3D surface models. **Line models** are needed when line elements are being used in engineering simulations. The important shell and beam engineering bending models are supported in Workbench DesignModeler by providing for the DesignModeler creation of surface models subsequently analyzed using ANSYS plate element technology and by the creation of line models to which beam cross sections are attached. Planar surfaces are also used to support analysis of **Plane Stress**, **Plane Strain** and **Axisymmetric** modeling.

3-6 TUTORIAL 3B – PLANAR SURFACE MODELS

We will use the L section solid of Tutorial 3A to create a planar surface model in this tutorial. Later we will use this same solid to create a three-dimensional surface model.

1. **Start DesignModeler** and **Open the file for Tutorial 3A.** The part is 15 x 25 x 2 x 10 mm long.

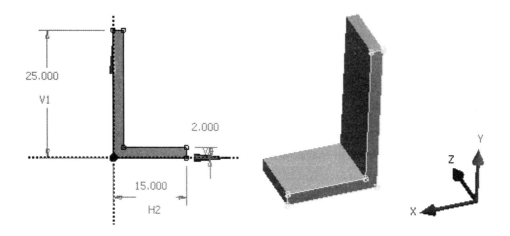

Figure 3-16 L-shaped section.

2. **Select the sketch in the tree outline**

3. **Concept > Surfaces from Sketches**

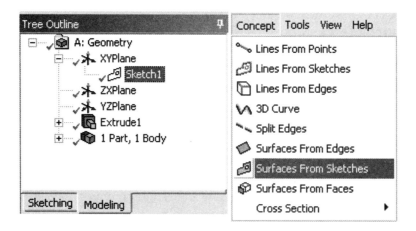

Figure 3-17 Surfaces from sketches.

4.   Details of SurfaceSk1; Base Objects > Apply, Thickness > 1

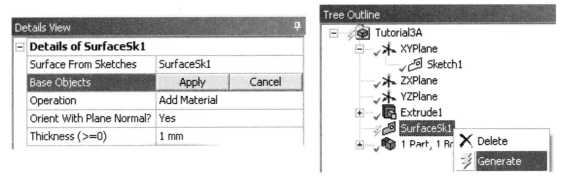

Figure 3-18 Generate the surface.

5.   Right Click SurfaceSk1 > Generate

This creates the surface model, and the solid we started with is no longer needed and may be deleted.

6.   Select Extrude1 > Delete > OK

The surface model is shown in the figure to the right. Notice that no thickness is shown. However the 1 mm thickness we supplied will be carried as a constant into a selected analysis module.

7.   Save this model as T3C

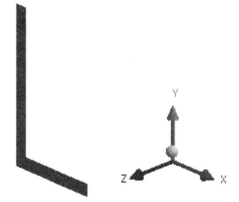

Figure 3-19 Surface model from Sk1.

Three-dimensional surface models can be developed from solids using the methods described next.

3-7   TUTORIAL 3C – 3D SURFACE MODELS

Again use the L section solid of Tutorial 3A.

1.   Start DesignModeler and Open the file for Tutorial 3A once again.

We want to capture the **middle surface** of the bracket.

2.   Tools > Mid-Surface

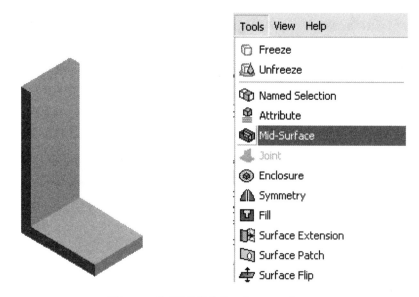

Figure 3-20 Mid-Surface tool.

3.   **Details of MidSurf2 > Face Pairs**

4.   Use **Ctrl Select** to sequentially pick **all** the **front and back** face **pairs** on the bracket model > **Apply**.

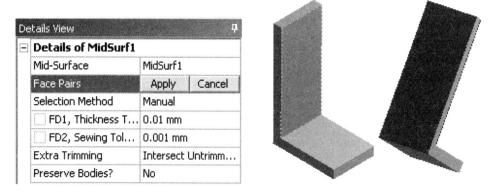

Figure 3-21 Mid-Surface face pairs.

5.   **Generate** ⟳ Generate   To create the surface.

Notice that this is a **three-dimensional surface model**.

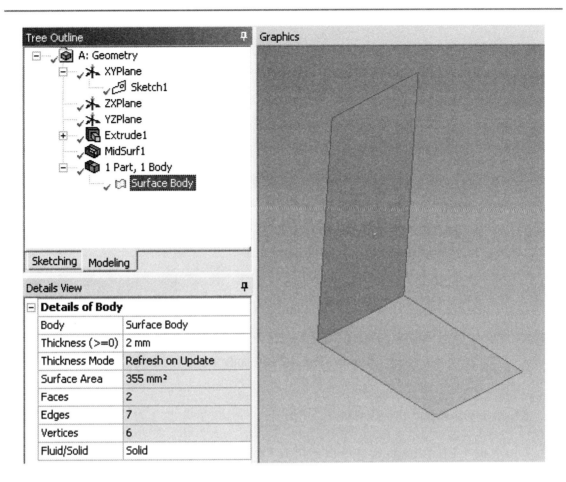

Figure 3-22 3D surface model of the L shaped section.

The **thickness of the Surface Body** is independent of the solid whose mid surface was used and is set by the user in **Details of Body** box as shown above. This thickness value (2 mm in our example) is carried into the analysis systems modules and is used for the calculations there. More detail on this is given in Chapter 8.

3-8 TUTORIAL 3D – LINE BODY MODELS

In the final tutorial of this chapter we develop a line body model to which a cross section is assigned. This model is then used in the analysis module to compute structural response using beam element modeling.

1.   **Start** an **instance of Workbench** and **Set** the **units** to **U.S.Engineering.**

2.   **In DesignModeler sketch on the XY Plane.**and use lines to **Sketch a portal 120 inches high** and **72 inches wide** (two verticals and one horizontal line across the top). See the next figure.

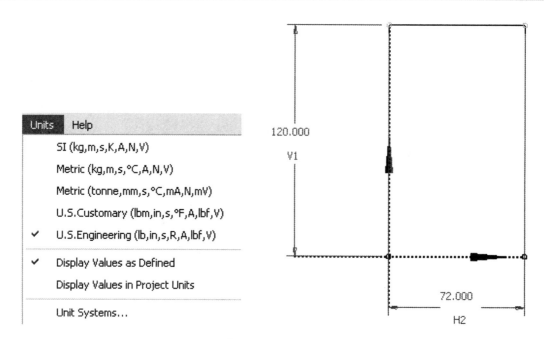

Figure 3-23 Portal.

3.   **Modeling > Select the Sketch**

4.   **Concept > Lines from Sketches > Base Objects > Apply** (The sketch is the base object.)

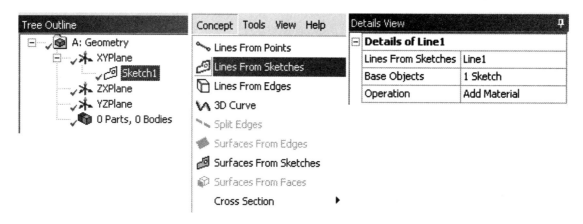

Figure 3-24 Lines from sketches.

5.   **Generate** This generates the line body. Next we **assign a cross section** to this line.

6.   **Concept > Cross Section > Channel**

We take the default size which is the **3 x 6 x 1 inch section** shown below and **assign it to the Line Body** as shown in the second figure below. **Line Body > Details > Cross Sctn.**

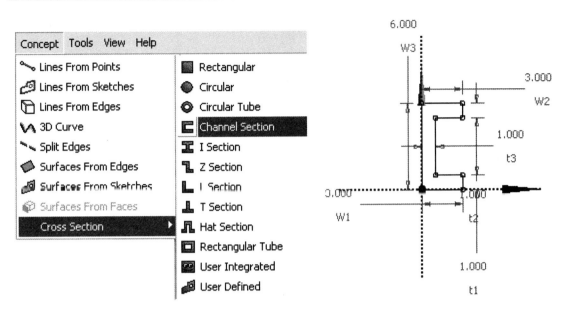

Figure 3-25 Channel section.

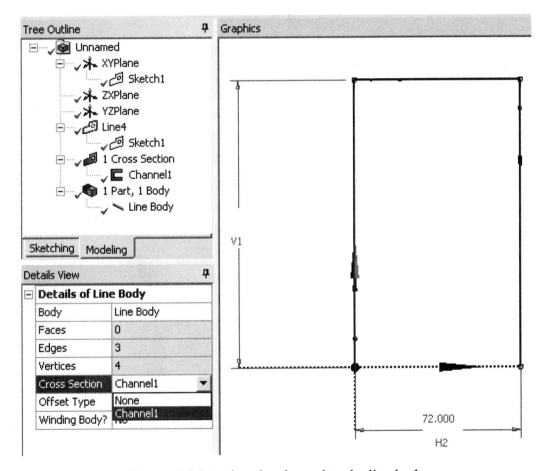

Figure 3-26 Assign the channel to the line body.

7.   **View > Show Cross Section Solids** (Displays the orientation of the section.)

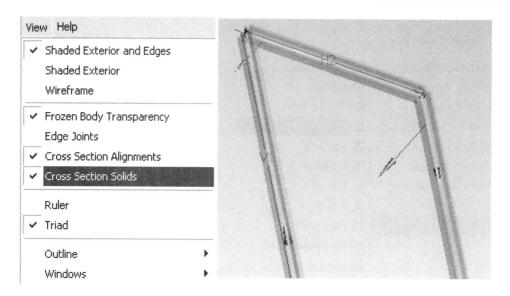

Figure 3-27 Show cross section.

The arrow normal to the portal plane (green on your screen) is aligned with the long edge of the channel cross section. Display the section orientation: **Uncheck Cross Section Alignments.**

To adjust the orientation of the top beam select as follows.

8.   **Turn on** the **Edge Selection Filter** and **Pick the Top Line-Body Edge. Reverse Orientation? > Yes**

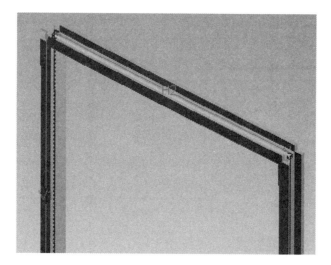

Figure 3-28 Close-up of section orientation.

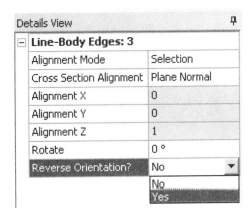

Figure 3-29 Alignment options.

Figure 3-30 Reverse orientation of top cross section.

The adjustment options shown in Figure 3-29 can be used in a number of ways to obtain proper beam cross section orientation for the problem at hand. Some experimentation may be helpful.

9.   Save your work.

This Line-Body model can be expanded using the sketching methods described earlier to add more elements and dimensionality to the model. We add vertical and horizontal lines sketched in the YZ Plane and a Concept > 3D Curve diagonal line joining the two outer vertices. This modification is shown in the following figure.

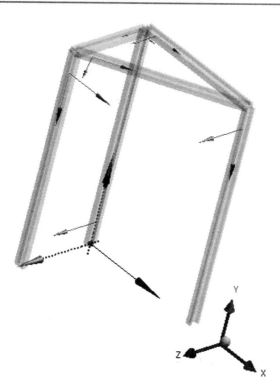

Figure 3-31 Expanded line-body model.

In Chapter 8 we will attach this model in the ANSYS analysis system to analyze the structure using beam elements.

Line bodies can also be created by connecting points that are entered from a text file. First **create a text file** with your list of points as shown below. The first entry is the **Group number** followed by **Point number**, then **X, Y** and **Z coordinates**.

```
1  1  0.0  0.0  0.0
1  2  2.5 -2.0  1.5
1  3 -1.5  3.2  2.1
etc.
```

Figure 3-32 Text file of points.

Use the **Point** icon from the toolbar Point to open the **Details** box below and **Generate** Generate to **Read** them into DM. Finally **Concept > Lines from Points**, (Click point to point) **Apply** and **Generate** to create your line-body model.

Details of Point1	
Point	Point1
Type	Construction Point
Definition	From Coordinates File
Coordinates File	C:\Doc...\node_points.txt
Tolerance	Normal

Figure 3-33 Locate and read points.

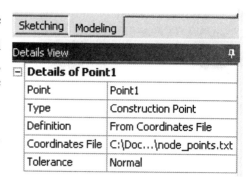

3-9 SUMMARY

Chapter 3 tutorials introduce the use of DesignModeler parameters and briefly discuss how to make use of other CAD systems and how to create models that are not solid models (lines and surfaces) for use in down-stream analysis.

3-10 PROBLEMS

3-1 Create parameter relations for the model of Problem 2-4 so that the height of the model is 6 times the wall thickness and the exterior radius is 3 times the wall thickness. The wall thickness and interior fillet remain unchanged. (See **Figure 5-1**) Are there size changes that produce invalid solid models?

3-2 Parameterize any of the DesignModeler parts created earlier in your study and examine the effect on the dependent parameters of changing a base dimension value. Are there size changes that produce invalid solid models?

3-3 Create parameter relations for the model of Problem 2-6 so that the large hole is placed at half the height of the part and always centered. The other dimensions remain unchanged. (See **Figure 8-20**) Are there size changes that produce invalid solid models?

3-4 Import an IGES or STEP file from another CAD system. If one is not available, export and save an IGES or STEP file from DesignModeler, start a new DesignModeler session and try importing that IGES or STEP file.

3-5 If another CAD system is available, use DesignModeler to attach the geometry for a part that is in an active session of that CAD system.

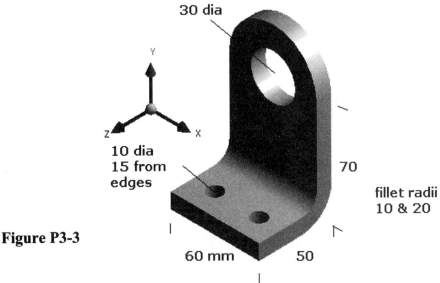

Figure P3-3

NOTES:

- Statical structural
    - Full body analysis
        assignment 9-11
    - Surface body
        assignment 14

option

Line body

- Thermal stress analysis
    - full assignment 13 [7B]
    - suface [7G]

- Modal analysis [9B]
    assignment 15

- linear Buckling [9F]
    assignment 15

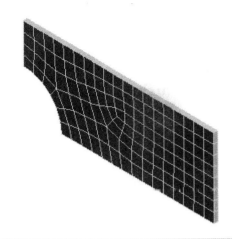

Chapter 4

ANSYS Mechanical I

4-1 OVERVIEW

ANSYS Workbench provides tools for the user to analyze the behavior of **Electric, Fluid, Magnetic, Mechanical, Thermal** systems and problems where more than one physical behavior is considered. In this Chapter we consider

♦ Stress response of a plate with a central hole.

♦ Stress response of a plate with various FEM mesh densities.

♦ The use of convergence criteria for controlling solution accuracy.

4-2 INTRODUCTION

Evaluating the response of a mechanical part or system in Workbench involves accessing the Geometry, assigning the Materials, applying the Loadings and Displacement Boundary Conditions, Solving the system Equations, Reviewing/Reporting the Results, and Updating the model if desired. An outline of this process is shown below.

1.   **Create and Attach problem Geometry.**

2.   **Assign Materials.**

3.   **Establish Contact Conditions if applicable.**

4.   **Preview the FEM Mesh and set up Mesh Controls if desired.**

5.   **Apply Loadings and Displacement Boundary Conditions.**

6.   **Select Results to be computed and displayed.**

7.   **Solve the system governing equations.**

8.   **Review the Results.**

9.   **Set problem Parameters if desired.**

10. **Create Reports of the response if appropriate.**

11. **Update the CAD model if necessary.**

To develop confidence in the process we start in Tutorial 4A by solving a simple structural static mechanical response problem. In this problem we can check the maximum stress result separately by a hand calculation.

4-3   TUTORIAL 4A – PLATE WITH CENTRAL CIRCLUAR HOLE

In this tutorial we will use **ANSYS Static Structural Analysis** to compute the maximum deflection and stress in a thin **steel** plate with a central hole. Its dimensions are **1000 mm long, 400 mm high** and **10 mm thick**. The central circular hole is **200 mm in diameter** as shown in the figure below. The plate is loaded in the long direction by a tensile force of **100 kN**.

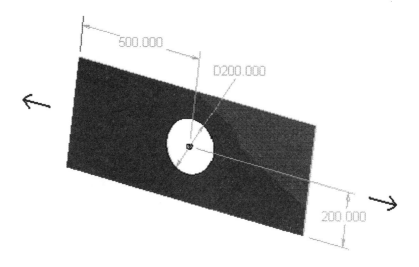

Figure 4-1 Thin plate with central hole.

First we need a **solid model of the plate**, and this can be created with **DesignModeler** or **another solid modeling system**. Since the central horizontal and vertical axes of the plate are on planes of plate geometry symmetry as well as loading symmetry, we need analyze only a quadrant of the part to obtain the stress distribution.

Use your solid modeler to trim the model to a quadrant as shown next.

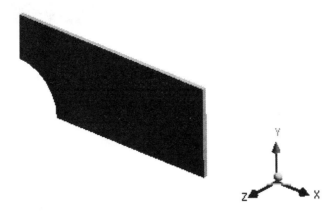

Figure 4-2 Quadrant of plate.

We follow the steps outlined above skipping those not needed in this tutorial.

In working through this and all the other tutorials keep in mind that your **results may vary slightly** due to sight difference in generated meshes.

1.   **START UP:** > Start **ANSYS Workbench,** begin a **new Project.**

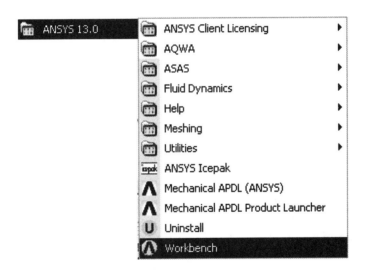

Figure 4-3 Starting ANSYS Workbench in Windows.

Double click ⬦ **Geometry** under **Toolbox** > **Component Systems** to initiate the geometry object in the **Project Schematic.**

See next figure.

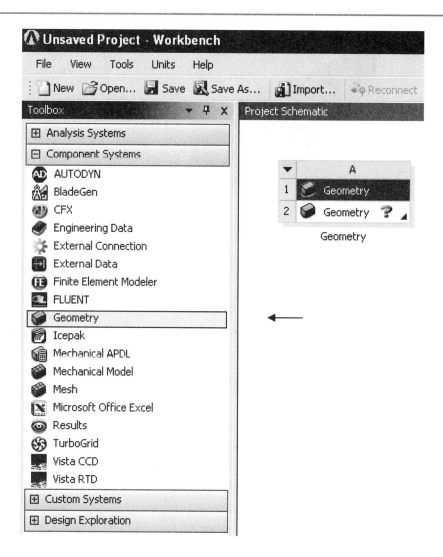

Figure 4-4 Project Schematic details.

The question mark indicates that **cell A-2** is incomplete.

2.   Select the **small blue triangle** for additional information. Click anywhere in the schematic to close the information box.

Select a folder in a convenient location on your storage device and **use Save As …** to **name** the project **T4A**. The project title, T4A, is displayed on the header as shown below and the **Workbench** project file **T4A.wbpj** and folder **T4A_files** are created in the selected workspace. Take a minute to find and verify this.

There are a number of ways to create and access geometry for your project. We discuss several, (**A., B., C., D., E.**) in what follows.

A. >> Create New Geometry in **Design Modeler: Double click cell A2** to start **Design Modeler.** Select problem **length units** and proceed to create geometry as discussed in Chapters 1 – 3. Save your DM work when you are finished.

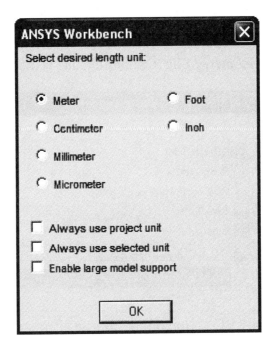

Figure 4-5 A >> Start new geometry in DesignModeler and set units.

B. >> Access Previously Created Geometry in **Design Modeler: Double click cell A2** to start **Design Modeler.**

File > Load DesignModeler Database (See the next figure.)

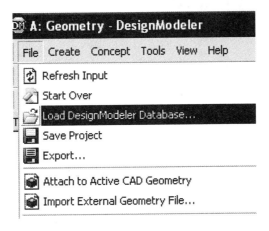

Figure 4-6 B >> Loading existing DM file.

C. >> Access Geometry Previously Created and stored using **another solid modeler:** **(CATIA, Pro/ENGINEER, SolidWorks, etc) Double click cell A2** to start **Design Modeler.**

File > Import External Geometry File (Options include **IGES** and **STEP** formats) (See the next figure.)

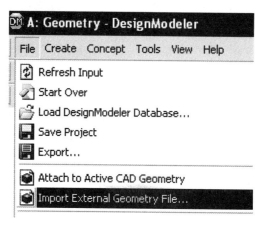

Figure 4-7 BC >> Importing from an alternate format.

This process starts the alternate solid modeler, loads that modeler's file, transfers the geometry to DesignModeler, and closes the alternate solid modeler.

D. >> Access Geometry in Active CAD system: Double click cell A2 to start **Design Modeler.**

File > Attach to Active CAD Geometry

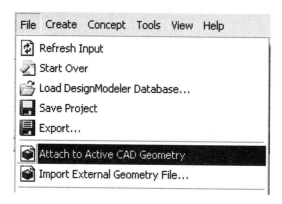

Figure 4-8 D >> Attach to Active CAD Geometry.

E. >> Start Workbench from your **alternate Solid Modeler.** An example of this using **Pro/ENGINEER** is shown below. Note the Pro/E icon is shown in cell A2 in the Workbench Project Schematic.

Double click cell A2 to start **DesignModeler**, then use **Generate** ⌇Generate to attach the Pro/E geometry.

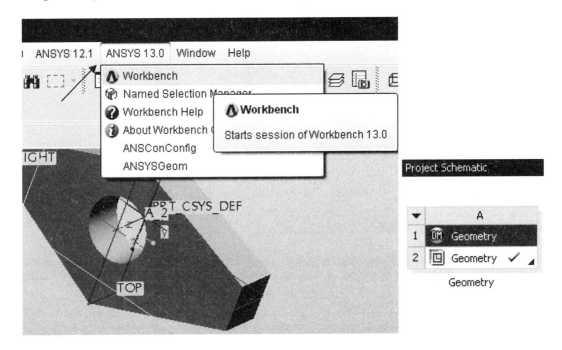

Figure 4-9 E >> Starting Workbench from Pro/ENGINEER.

3. Getting **back to Tutorial 4A**, with the geometry attached, **Double Click Toolbox > Analysis Systems > Static Structural** to add the analysis to the **Project Schematic.** (Or **drag** it from the Analysis Systems column to the Schematic.)

Figure 4-10 Adding Static Structural Analysis from the Toolbox.

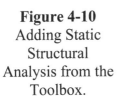

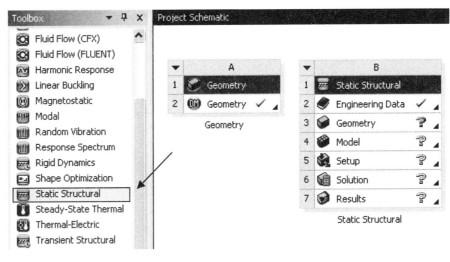

4.   To **share** the geometry, **Left click** on **DM Geometry** in **cell A2** and **drag** it to **Static Structural cell B3**.

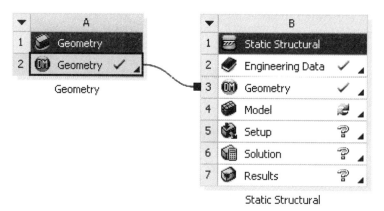

Figure 4-11 Sharing geometry.

5.   **Double Click** on **Model** in **cell B4**.

The Workbench display now shows the **Static Structural Analysis** that is associated with this **Project**, and the tree structure on the left contains project items that include **Model**, **Geometry**, and **Mesh**. See the figure below.

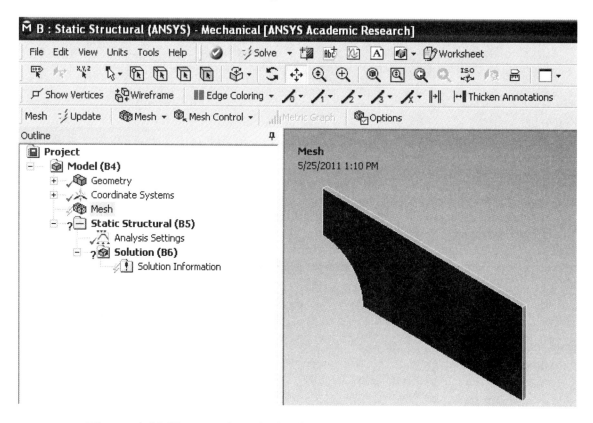

Figure 4-12 Plate quadrant in Static Structural Mechanical module.

Since the geometry was created using mm, the length units for the simulation should be mm also. **Check the units** using the **Units** pull-down menu. **Units > Metric (mm, kg, N, s, mV, mA)**

6.   **Highlight Material** in the **Details of "T4A"** window.

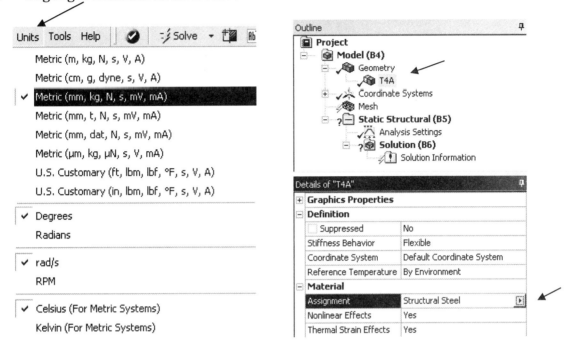

Figure 4-13 Check Units and Material assignment.

To return to the **Project Schematic, Select T4A – Workbench** from the programs running shown in the taskbar at the bottom of the screen.

Figure 4-14 Workbench elements shown in Taskbar.

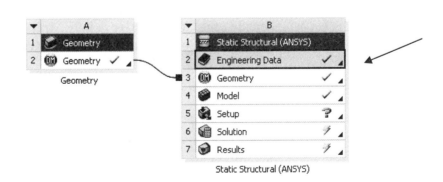

Figure 4-15 Project Schematic.

7.   Double click **Engineering Data, cell B2** to view the **Material Properties Data for Structural Steel,** the **default material** that has been assigned to this part.

Be sure **View** > **Properties & Outline** and **Engineering Data Sources** are turned on. **Select General Materials > Structural Steel**

	A	B	C
	Properties of Outline Row 3: Structural Steel		
1	Property	Value	Unit
2	🗗 Density	7850	kg m^-3 ▼
3	⊟ 🗗 Isotropic Secant Coefficient of Thermal Expansion		
4	🗗 Coefficient of Thermal Expansion	1.2E-05	C^-1 ▼
5	🗗 Reference Temperature	22	C ▼
6	⊟ 🗗 Isotropic Elasticity		
7	Derive from	Young's M. ▼	
8	Young's Modulus	2E+11	Pa ▼
9	Poisson's Ratio	0.3	
10	Bulk Modulus	1.6667E+11	Pa
11	Shear Modulus	7.6923E+10	Pa
12	⊟ 🗗 Alternating Stress Mean Stress	▦ Tabular	
13	Scale	1	
14	Offset	0	Pa
15	Interpolation	Log-Log ▼	
16	⊞ 🗗 Strain-Life Parameters		
24	🗗 Tensile Yield Strength	2.5E+08	Pa ▼
25	🗗 Compressive Yield Strength	2.5E+08	Pa ▼
26	🗗 Tensile Ultimate Strength	4.6E+08	Pa ▼
27	🗗 Compressive Ultimate Strength	0	Pa ▼

Figure 4-16 Material properties for structural steel.

Note that structural steel has **Tensile** and **Compressive Yield Strengths** of **250 MPa**. And that no value has been assigned to the **Compressive Ultimate Strength**.

8.   **Select Return to Project** (Top of screen) ⬅Return to Project .

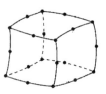

The Mesh item in the project tree has a lighting bolt symbol next to it indicating that the finite element mesh for this simulation has not yet been created. Workbench simulation will automatically develop a finite element mesh appropriate to the problem.

9.   **MESH:** Right click **Mesh** and select **Generate Mesh**

The default mesh that is created consists of a little over one hundred three-dimensional **20node brick elements** (previous figure) as shown below.

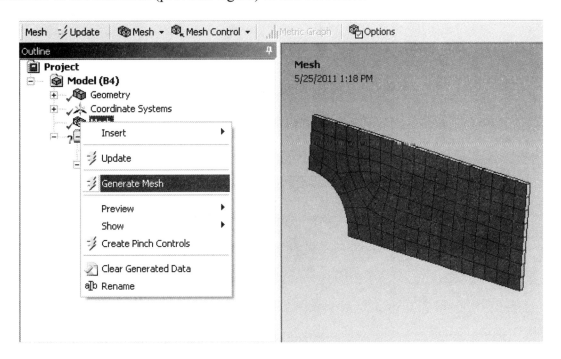

Figure 4-17 Meshing the geometry.

10.   Select **Static Structural (B5)** from the Outline tree structure (next Figure). The Environment displays loadings and boundary condition options available for this analysis.

Since only the upper half of the plate is being analyzed, apply **a Force of 50 kN** to the right end surface.

11.   **APPLY LOADINGS:** Click **Environment > Loads > Force**

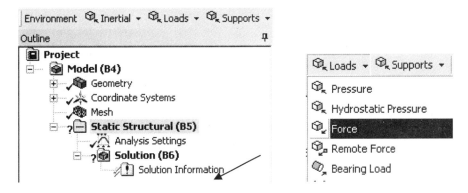

Figure 4-18 Structural loads menu.

Be sure that the **Face** selection filter is highlighted 🔲 and **click on the area** on the right end of the solid model.

12.   **Geometry > Apply** (Note: It's easy to forget this step.)

13.   **Define** (the force) **by** (X Y Z) **Components, X Component = 50 kN**

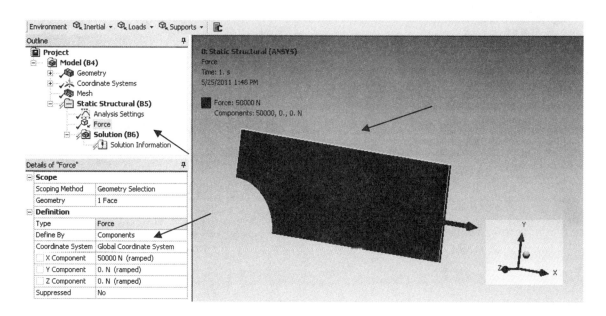

Figure 4-19 Tensile loading.

Next apply the **displacement constraints**; rotate the plate so that you can see the bottom, and small end. These are surfaces on planes of symmetry and no point on these surfaces can move across the plane of symmetry. Symmetry requires that we constrain the displacements perpendicular to these surfaces. We can use the **Frictionless Support** condition to do that. We also restrain the **back surface** also so as to prevent rigid body motion in a direction perpendicular to the plane of the plate. See the figure below.

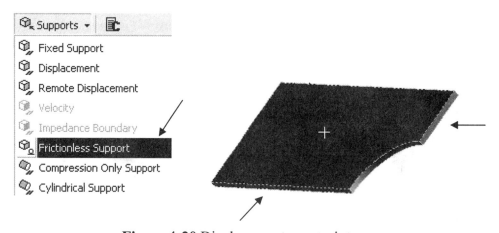

Figure 4-20 Displacement constraints.

14.   **Environment > Supports > Frictionless Support**

15.   **Ctrl > Left Click** to select the **three** surfaces > **Apply**

Details of "Frictionless Support"		卑
⊟ **Scope**		
Scoping Method	Geometry Selection	
Geometry	3 Faces	
⊟ **Definition**		
Type	Frictionless Support	
Suppressed	No	

Figure 4-21 Frictionless Support constraints.

Check your work by clicking on each of the items under Environment in the model tree to be sure the loadings and constraints are applied as desired. Or click **Static Structural** to see all of the constraints you have applied.

If you find something wrong, just highlight the item in the model tree and edit it in the 'Details' box to correct the error, or Right Click, delete the item from the outline tree and apply the condition again.

(Note that the back face is not really a plane of symmetry. To be absolutely correct we should have sliced down through the 10 mm thickness and analyzed an octant instead of a quadrant. However since the 10 mm dimension is so small in comparison with the other dimensions, there is little error in the approach we used.)

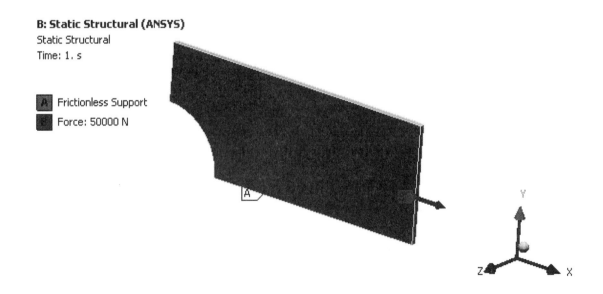

Figure 4-22 Environment settings.

To complete the model building process we need to specify what **result** quantity or quantities we would like to have calculated and displayed. In this problem we are most interested in the **stress** and **deformation** in the **X Axis direction**.

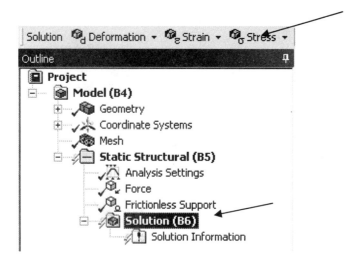

Figure 4-23 Solution result options menu.

16.   Solution > Stress > Normal > Orientation > X Axis

Also select **Deformation** and insert the **Directional Deformation** in the **X Axis**.

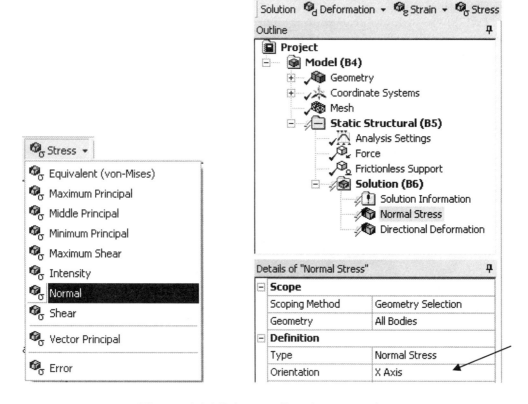

Figure 4-24 Select X-direction normal stress output.

Notice that Solution, Normal Stress, and Directional Displacement items have lightning bolt indicators meaning that we need to highlight one or the other and select 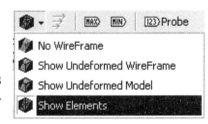 to complete the simulation solution.

17. Solve

The solution progress is shown in the **ANSYS Workbench Solution Status** window.

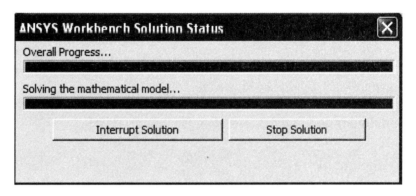

Figure 4-25 Solution status.

When the solution is found, click on the normal stress to view the computed stress results.

18. Solution > Stress > Normal Stress (In the graphics window - Right click > View > Front; Use the pull-down menu to **Show Elements**)

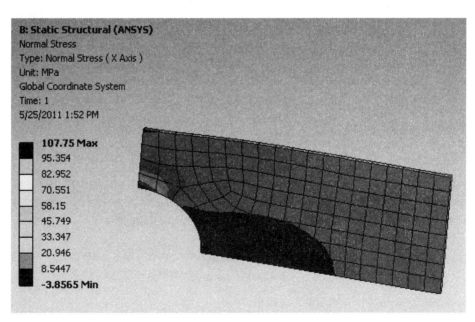

Figure 4-26 X direction normal stress.

The solution for the X direction normal stress shows a **maximum value** of **107 MPa**. This value is well below the material yield stress of 250 MPa, so the elastic solution that we have performed is valid.

To check this result, find the stress concentration factor for this problem in a text or reference book or from a web site. For the geometry of this example we find $K_t = 2.17$. We can compute the maximum stress using $(K_t)(load)/(net\ cross\ sectional\ area)$. Using the whole bar and a loading of 100 kN we obtain:

$$\sigma_{x\,MAX} = 2.17 * F * /[(0.4 - 0.2) * 0.01] = 109\,MPa$$

The computed maximum value is **107 MPa** which is less than **two per cent in error** (assuming that the published value of K_t is exact).

The **maximum deformation** in the X direction is about 0.08 mm.

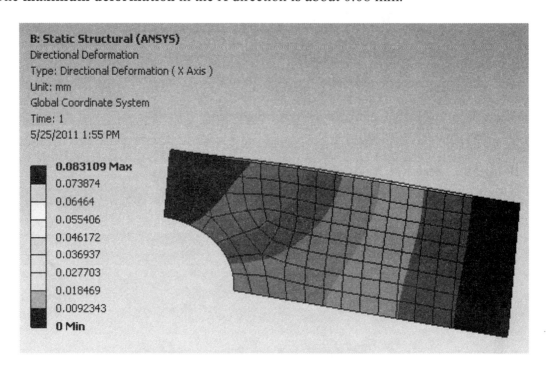

Figure 4-27 X direction deformation.

Before we leave this tutorial let's compute and display the stress **error estimate** for this problem. Insert a stress error in the solution item in the project tree.

19.   **Solution > Stress > Error > Solve**   Solve

Computed results are shown in the next figure.

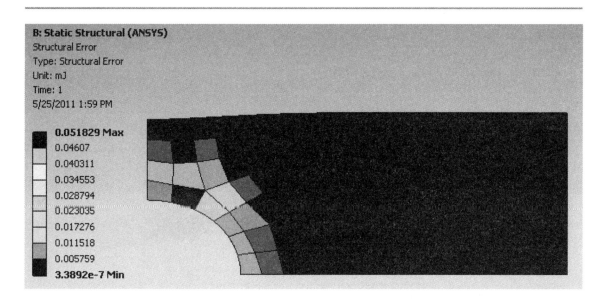

Figure 4-28 Computed structural error estimates.

The error estimates shown above can be used to help identify regions of potentially high error in the solution and thus show where the model might benefit from a more refined mesh. These error estimates are used in Workbench automatic adaptive meshing and convergence procedures we discuss later.

For now we note that the Structural Errors shown are **error estimates** based upon the difference between a **smoothed stress distribution** computed for the object and the stresses calculated by the finite element method for **each element in the mesh**. The data are expressed in an energy format (energy is nonnegative) so that the sign of the difference between the estimated stress and the computed stress does not influence the results. The estimated error is displayed for each element.

For accurate solutions the difference between the smoothed stress and the element stress is small or zero, so small values of Structural Error are good. We know the above solution is reasonably accurate because we compared our result with tabulated results. The small error estimates shown above reflect this.

To **improve the accuracy** we'll generate a model with more elements. There are many ways to control the mesh in Workbench. In what follows we use one of the sizing options.

20.   **Mesh > Details of Mesh > Relevance Center > Medium** (Coarse is the default.) **Solve** again.

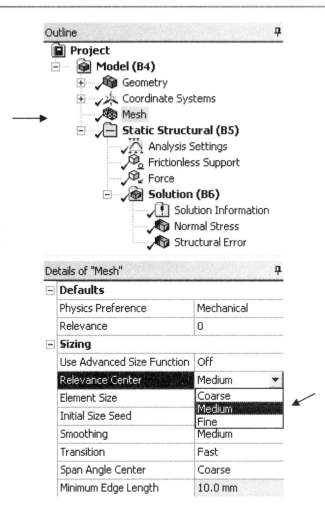

Figure 4-29 Relevance Center mesh settings.

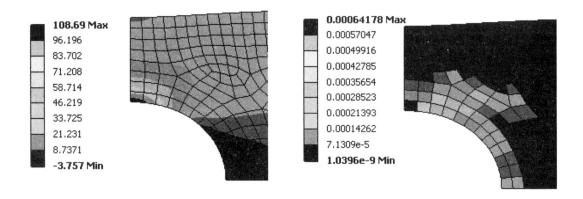

Figure 4-30 Stress and error estimates based on a detailed mesh.

21.   **Repeat** this process using the **Fine Mesh** setting.

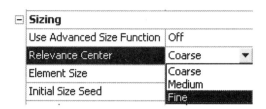

Figure 4-31 Relevance Center Fine mesh settings.

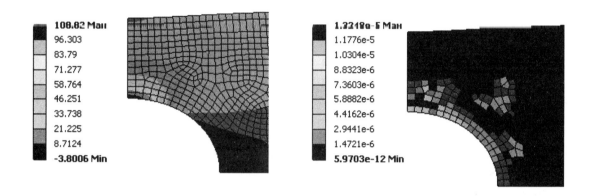

Figure 4-32 Stress and error estimates based on the fine mesh.

22. **Let's compute another solution** for a **mesh** that is **coarser** than the first one. Set the **Element Size = 50 mm** and remesh. We get the results shown below.

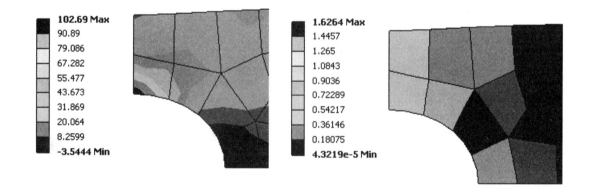

Figure 4-33 Stress and error estimates based a coarse mesh.

These results are summarized in the table below. Note that with the finer meshes we obtain a maximum stress of about 109 MPa.

Results Summary

Number of Elements	Maximum Deformation in X direction	Maximum Stress in X direction
36	0.0831	102.7
137	0.0831	107.8
511	0.0831	108.8
3182	0.0831	108.8

It is important to note the **approximate nature** of the **Finite Element Method** and the **convergence** of the **stress results with mesh refinement** as illustrated in the above table. Note that with a coarse mesh you can get results that are **in error**, only about 6 per cent in this case, but don't accept results from an initial mesh without question. (Set the element size to 75 mm, and see what you get.)

Also note that the tabulated **displacement results** show no change to three significant figures indicating that the displacements converge more rapidly than the stresses. This is usually the case. The strains (hence stresses) are the spatial directives of the displacement distributions within the object, i.e., $\varepsilon_x = \partial u / \partial x$, etc. (See the Introductory chapter)

We will do two more experiments before moving on. Return to the **50 mm mesh** and change the **stress plotting option**.

23.   Select Normal Stress > Display Option > Unaveraged. Recalculate the solution.

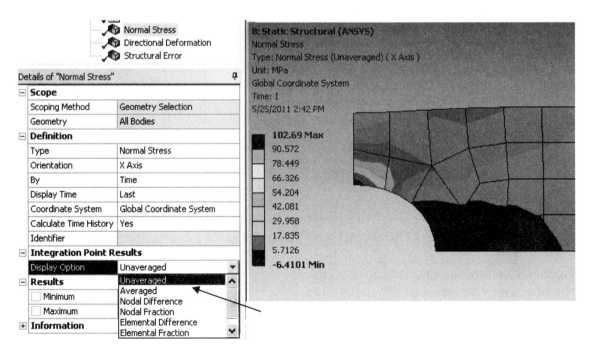

Figure 4-34 Unaveraged stress plot.

The figure above is not much different from the previous stress plot except there are some small discontinuities in the low stress region.

Let's now use a different element. In the mesh details box, drop the **element midside nodes**.

24.   Select Mesh > Advanced > Element Midside Nodes > Dropped

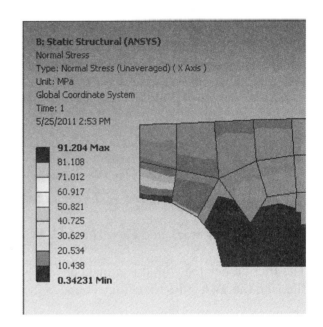

Figure 4-35 Stress results found using 8-node brick elements.

In the figure above note the maximum stress is only **91 MPa** (a 13 per cent error) and the stresses are discontinuous at many element boundaries. We **should not have a discontinuous stress distribution** in a uniform solid. What's up?

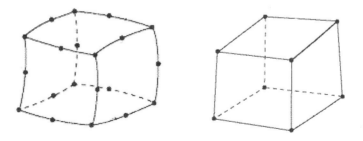

Figure 4-36 20 node and 8 node solid elements.

The previous results were all calculated using brick elements **with midside nodes**, that's **20 nodes per element**. These last results were found using bricks with **nodes only at the**

corners, 8-node elements. As discussed in the Introduction, higher order elements (those with midside nodes) generally give better results because of the better representation of the displacements, strains and stresses within the element. That's what we see here.

At the completion of the solution, the project schematic shows all items checked off in the Static Structural matrix as shown below.

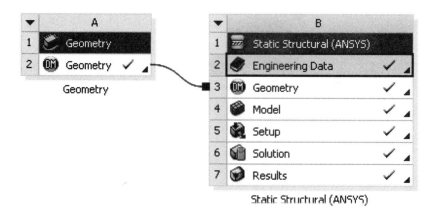

Figure 4-37 Project Schematic after solution.

25.   Save your work and **close the T4A Workbench Project.**

The files associated with this project are shown in figure below. **T4A.wbpj** is the project file, and the **T4A_files directory** contains the supporting files as shown.

Figure 4-38 Files stored after Workbench Project has been closed.

The figure above shows the directory and files associated with this project. Take a minute to verify this.

4-4 TUTORIAL 4B – PLATE WITH CENTRAL SQUARE HOLE

Suppose we take the plate of Tutorial 4A and replace the circular hole with a **200 mm square hole**. The upper right quadrant of the model is shown below.

1.   **Open a new Workbench Project; create the model shown below** and **save as T4B.**

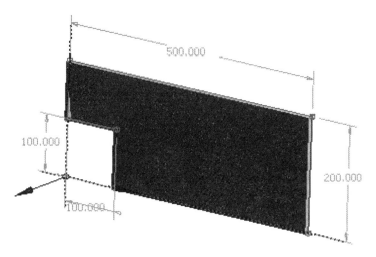

Figure 4-39 Plate with square hole.

2.   Start a new **Static Structural Analysis** using the quadrant of a plate with a square central cut out. **Share Geometry** and **Double Click Model** to start **Mechanical.**

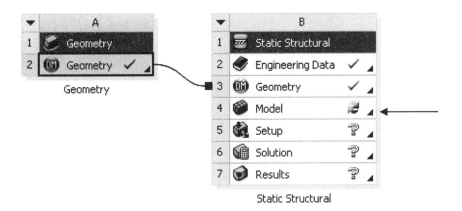

Figure 4-40 Project schematic.

3.   **Mesh > Generate Mesh** The next figure shows the default mesh for this problem.

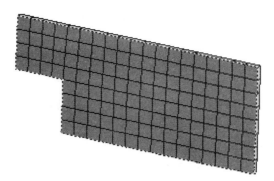

Figure 4-41 Default mesh for the plate with square hole.

The default mesh consists of 136 brick elements as shown above.

4.   **Apply the displacement boundary conditions** and **loading** as in **Tutorial T4A.**

Include the **X direction normal stress** in the computed quantities.

5.   **Solution > Stress > Normal > Details of "Normal Stress" > Orientation >
      X Axis**

6.   **Solve** *Solve* and view the normal stress solution. Also click the **Max** icon.

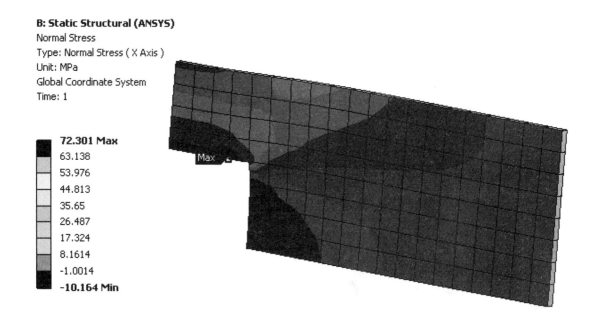

Figure 4-42 Normal stress in. the X direction.

7.   **Right click** and **select** the **front view**. The smooth stress contours show a
      maximum stress of around **72 MPa**.

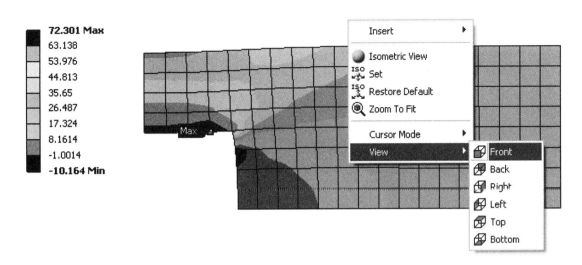

Figure 4-43 Normal stress for 25 mm elements.

The default mesh consists of elements that are 25 mm by 25 mm and 10 mm thick. Suppose we reduce the element size and examine the effect on the computed stresses. In the outline tree click on **Mesh**, then in **Details of "Mesh" change** the **element size** from **25 mm** to **10 mm**.

8. **Mesh > Details of "Mesh"**

9. **Element Size > 10 mm**

Figure 4-44 Set the element size.

10.   Right click Mesh > Generate Mesh

The new mesh with 900 elements is shown below.

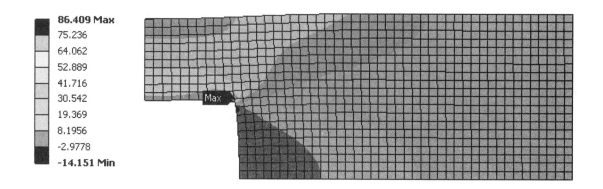

Figure 4-45 Normal stress for 10 mm elements

11.   Solve ⌐⧸Solve **and view the normal stress solution.**

The computed **maximum** normal stress is **86.4 MPa**, an increase of about **20 per cent**.

Now reduce the mesh size to **5 mm**. This creates a 7200 element mesh.

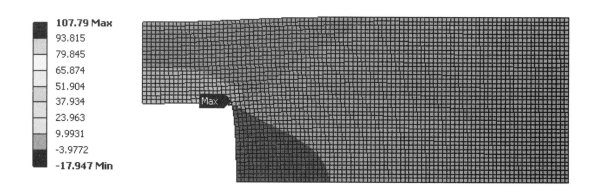

Figure 4-46 Normal stress for 5 mm elements.

The computed **maximum** normal stress is **107.8 MPa**, an increase of around **25 per cent**.

Finally, reduce the mesh size to **3 mm**, producing a model with over 41,000 elements

12.   Details of "Mesh" > Element Size > 3 mm

13.   Again **Solve** 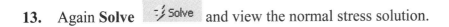 and view the normal stress solution.

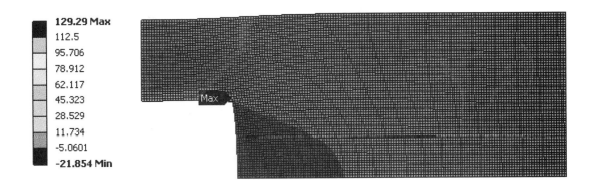

Figure 4-47 Normal stress for 3 mm elements.

The newly computed maximum normal stress in the X-direction is **129 MPa**, an increase over the previous value of **20 per cent**. So, **what is happening?**

The behavior of the maximum stress results we just computed are due to the **stress singularity** at the corner of the square hole. The corner has a zero radius of curvature where the two edges meet, and as the radius of an interior corner or other notch approaches zero, the computed stress approaches an **infinite value**.

If the material is ductile and the loads are static, the high stresses at this singularity may not be of concern in the actual use of the part. If the material is brittle **or** the loading is repetitive (fatigue situation), then it is **very important** to model the **actual geometry** and thus determine the correct stress value in the vicinity of the notch.

During manufacture of a real plate it would be difficult to make the edges of the hole meet with a zero radius at the corner, or it may be that a specific corner radius is needed for the function of the part. Suppose for our plate the actual **corner radius** is **15 mm.** Make this geometry change in the model of the plate or the solid modeler you are using.

14.   Return to the **Project Schematic** and **double click Geometry**. Working in DesignModeler we will add the fillet radius to a part created in Pro/E.

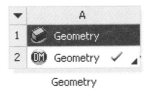

Figure 4-48 Project schematic view.

15. Select the **Edge Filter** 🔳, Click the interior **Corner Edge** and then select **Fixed Radius Blend** ◈ Blend **Enter 15 mm > Generate** ⌁ Generate

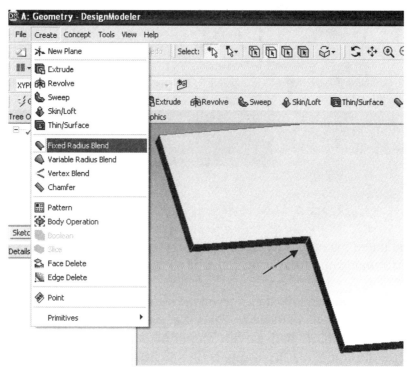

Figure 4-49 Part in DesignModeler.

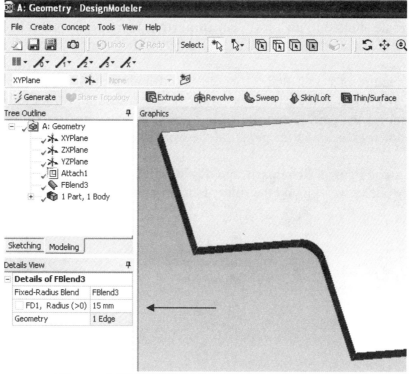

Figure 4-50 Updated DesignModeler geometry.

Now **update** the Static Structural Analysis model to the new geometry.

16.   Return to the **Project Schematic** view. Left click on the **small blue triangle** in **cell B4, Model.**

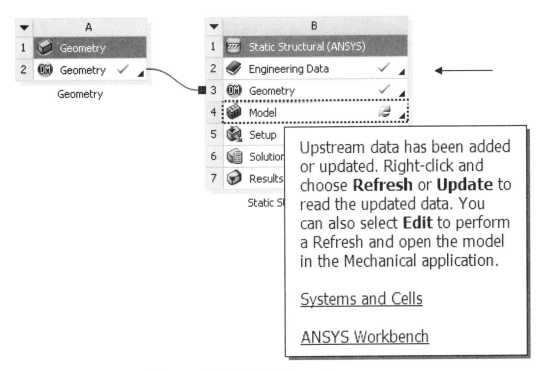

Figure 4-51 Model information screen.

17.   **Right Click in cell B4, Model** and Select **Update**.

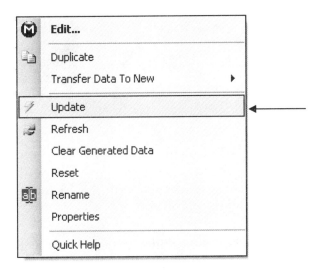

Figure 4-52 Update the model.

After the update is complete, return to the Static Structural 🅜 Mechanical screen.

18.   Reset the mesh **Relevance** to **Coarse** and **enter 0, return** for **Element Size** to reset to **Default**.

Sizing	
Use Advanced Size Function	Off
Relevance Center	Coarse
Element Size	Default
Initial Size Seed	Active Assembly
Smoothing	Medium
Transition	Fast
Span Angle Center	Coarse
Minimum Edge Length	10.0 mm

Figure 4-53 Reset element size.

The project now is updated; the material, load and frictionless supports remain the same; the analysis proceeds as before.   Solve

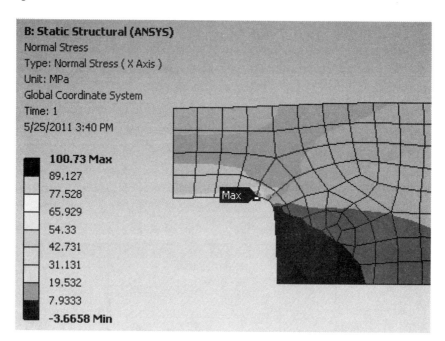

Figure 4-54 Default mesh for modified geometry.

The computed maximum stress associated with the 15 mm corner radius is about **101 MPa**.

We can control the accuracy of the solution manually as we did in previous examples or we can request an **automatic iterative solution** process to be employed that will use models with successively smaller element sizes while monitoring the change in the requested solution quantity. This is essentially an automation of what we did manually earlier.

Select maximum Normal Stress as the quantity to monitor during iterative solution.

19. Right click **Normal Stress** > **Insert** > Left click **Convergence**

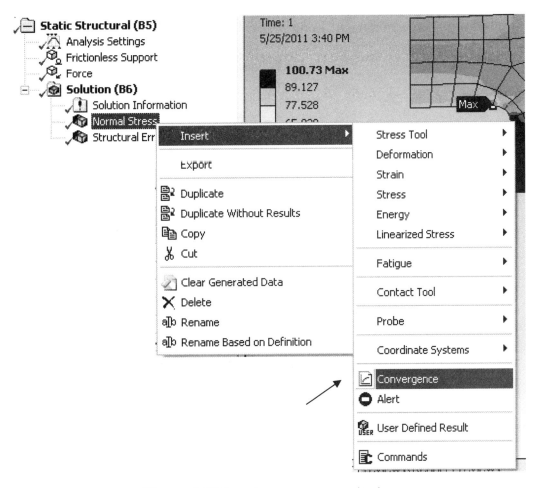

Figure 4-55 Insert convergence criterion.

Define the allowable change in maximum Normal Stress between solutions.

20. **Details of "Convergence" > Allowable Change > 1 per cent**

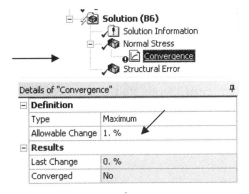

Figure 4-56 Allowable change in normal stress.

Define the default number of mesh refinements and depth (refinement gradations).

21.   Solution > Max Refinement Loops > 4;   Refinement Depth > 2

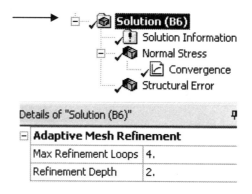

Figure 4-57 Adaptive refinement parameters.

22.   Right click Solution or Normal Stress > Solve

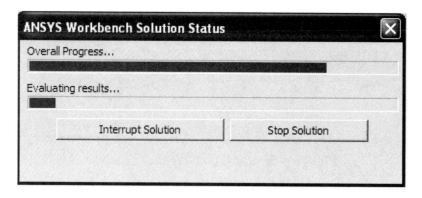

Figure 4-58 Solution status.

23.   Once the solution process has finished, click on Convergence.

The convergence results shown in the next figure are displayed. The model is refined from 1088 nodes and 135 elements to one with 69,225 nodes and 46,623 elements. The maximum normal stress in the X-direction changes from **101 MPa** to about **123 MPa**, a total change of about **22 per cent.** Note that the repeated solution continues until the **change** in maximum normal stress is less than 1 per cent as requested. See the next figure.

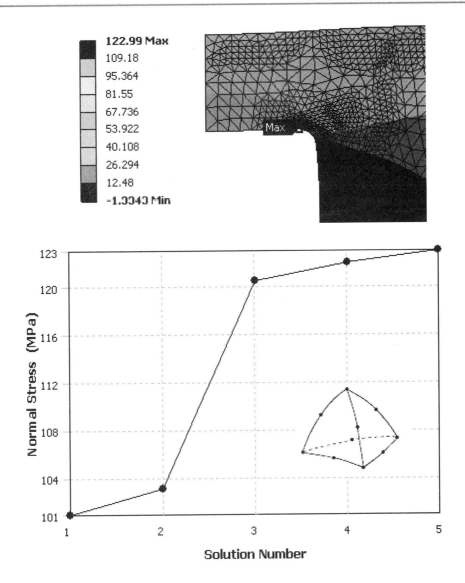

Figure 4-59 Final mesh and stress convergence history.

	Normal Stress (MPa)	Change (%)	Nodes	Elements
1	100.94		1088	135
2	103.13	2.1493	4569	2482
3	120.52	15.554	9290	5603
4	122.02	1.2363	26588	17241
5	122.99	0.79053	69225	46623

The convergence path could be altered by the choice of the mesh refinements. A uniform mesh refinement followed by a local refinement using this convergence object will likely produce different intermediate results. Experimentation and experience are important. Note also that for ease of meshing, the automatic meshing process changed to **ten-node tetrahedron elements**.

24. Save your work.

4-5   SUMMARY

The tutorials in Chapter 4 illustrate basic concepts of stress computation with Structrual Static Mechanical simulation coupled with ANSYS DesignModeler or another solid modeler. We note that computed values must be examined carefully to evaluate their accuracy and that manual or automatic **convergence studies** can and **should** be used to insure quality of results. **Don't accept** the results of the **first coarse mesh** you try.

In the next Chapter we will extend these ideas to more complex parts and introduce additional simulation modeling options.

4-6   PROBLEMS

4-1   Consider a thin structural steel plate such as the one shown below. Compute the **maximum normal stress** in the horizontal (X) direction if **100 kN tensile load** is applied to the left and right end surfaces. Compare your result with the value you compute using tabulated stress concentration factors for this geometry. Insert a convergence control to help access the accuracy of your solution.

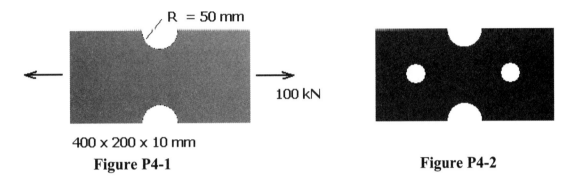

Figure P4-1   **Figure P4-2**

4-2   Place a 25 mm diameter hole 100 mm to left and to the right of the vertical centerline but on the horizontal centerline of the part in Problem 4-1. Find the magnitude and location of the **maximum normal stress**.

4-3   Consider the long, thin structural steel plate shown below, fixed at one end, free at the other. Apply a pressure on the upper edge and compute the **deflection** at the free end and **maximum bending stress** at the middle of the beam. Compare your result with the result you can compute from beam theory.

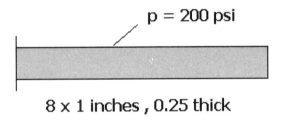

Figure P4-3

4-4   Repeat the problem described in Problem 4-3 but make the plate 1 x 1 x 0.25. Slender beam theory no longer applies to this geometry. Compare results to verify that.

Figure P4-4

4-5   Repeat the problem described in Problem 4-3 but place a 0.25 inch diameter hole at the center of the beam.

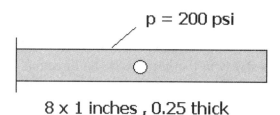

Figure P4-5

4-6 The central bore of the indexing wheel and the 8 slots are all 1.0 inch in diameter. The thickness is 0.5 inch and diameter D = 4 inches. Find the **maximum principal strain** in **pressurized indexing slot** if the applied pressure is 5,000 psi. Ignore the strains in the completely fixed central hole. Report the calculated decimal value and also report the result in terms of micro-strain, that is, the value computed multiplied by 10^6.

4-7 Repeat problem 4-8 but use vertical plane to slice off half of the geometry. Put frictionless supports on the exposed plane of symmetry.

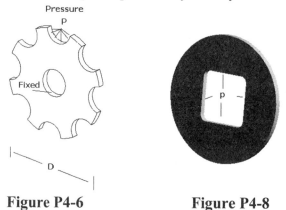

Figure P4-6   **Figure P4-8**

4-8 A 20 inch diameter cylinder has an 8 in square hole with 1.0 inch radius corner fillets. The thickness is 0.75 inch. Find the maximum values for **von Mises stress**, **principal stress**, **shear stress**, and **displacement** if the front and back surfaces have frictionless supports and the interior has a pressure of 7500 psi..

Chapter 5

ANSYS Mechanical II

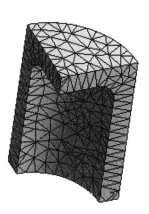

5-1 OVERVIEW

This chapter covers stress and deflection simulation response of some three-dimensional solids representative of typical mechanical parts. We consider the simulation of the following objects

♦ Pressure Vessel

♦ Angle Bracket

♦ Clevis Yoke

5-2 INTRODUCTION

The close integration with DesignModeler and other solid modeling tools makes ANSYS Mechanical particularly well suited to the analysis of solids. We consider a few typical examples in the tutorials that follow.

5-3 TUTORIAL 5A - CYLINDRICAL PRESSURE VESSEL

A steel pressure vessel with planar ends is subjected to an **internal pressure of 35 MPa**. The vessel has an **outer diameter of 200 mm**, an over-all **length of 400 mm** and a **wall thickness of 25 mm**. There is a **25 mm fillet radius** where the interior wall surface joins the end cap as shown in the figure below.

The vessel has a longitudinal axis of **rotational symmetry** and is also symmetric with respect to a plane passed through it at mid-height. Thus the analyst need consider only the **top** or **bottom half** of the **vessel**.

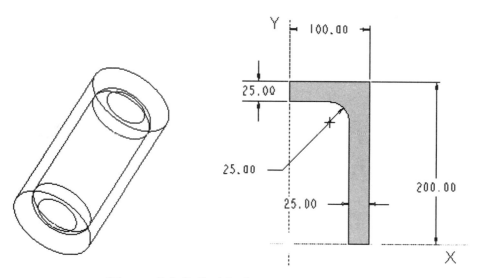

Figure 5-1 Cylindrical pressure vessel.

We will use a 90-degree segment of the solid model of the vessel for analysis. The symmetric nature of the geometry and loading means that displacements are zero in directions normal to the faces exposed by the vertical and horizontal cuts employed to create this one-eighth segment of the cylinder. Use ANSYS DesignModeler or other solid modeler to create a solid model of the upper portion of the vessel.

1. **Start ANSYS Workbench** and **DesignModeler. Create** or **attach the quadrant geometry,** and **Save** the **Project** using the name **T5A**

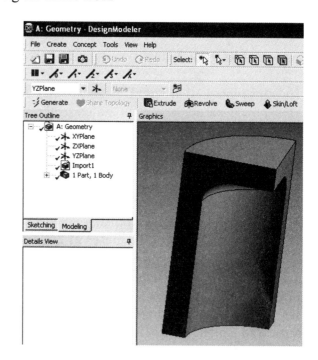

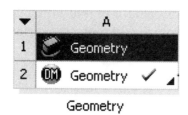

Figure 5-2 Project Schematic and quadrant of cylinder.

2.   Add **Static Structural** from the **Toolbox > Analysis Systems** and **Share** the
Geometry.   Double Click **Model.**

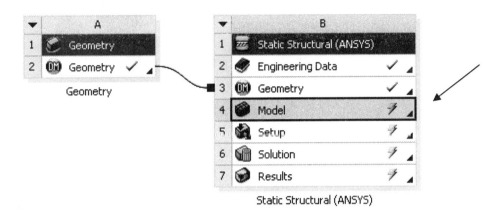

Figure 5-3 Project Schematic.

We will use the **default materials values for steel**. **Check the units settings**, then Right
click **Model (B4)** and **rename as T5A-Vessel**.

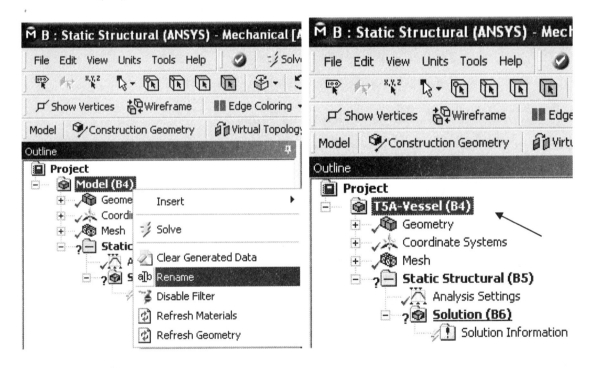

Figure 5-4 Rename Outline object.

3.   **Mesh > (right click) Generate Mesh**

The default mesh shown below is created. The default mesh uses tetrahedral elements and
this has only one element through the thickness. Let's replace it with a finer mesh.

4.   **Mesh > Right click > Clear Generated Data > Yes** (This removes the mesh.)

5.   **Details of Mesh > Sizing > Relevance Center > Medium.** Generate new mesh.

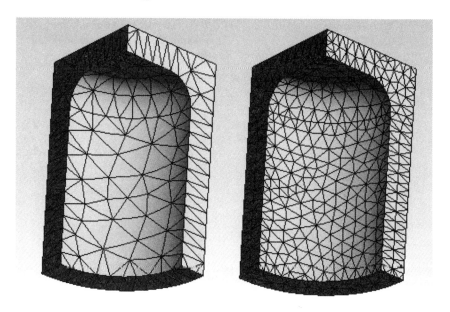

Figure 5-5 Initial and improved mesh.

Apply **Frictionless Support** boundary conditions on the planes of symmetry.

6.   **Environment > Supports > Frictionless Support**

7.   Select the **Three surfaces** on the planes of symmetry**. > Apply**

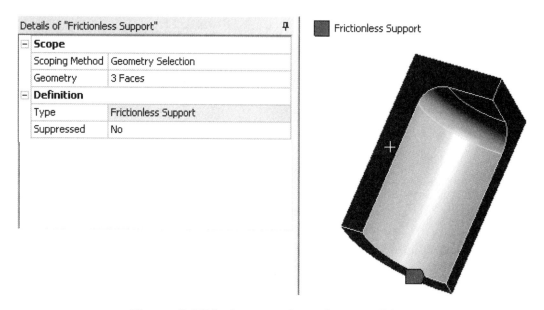

Figure 5-6 Displacement boundary conditions.

8.   **Environment > Loads > Pressure > Ctrl Select** all interior surfaces > **Details of "Pressure" > Apply**

9.   **Details of "Pressure" > Magnitude > 35 MPa**

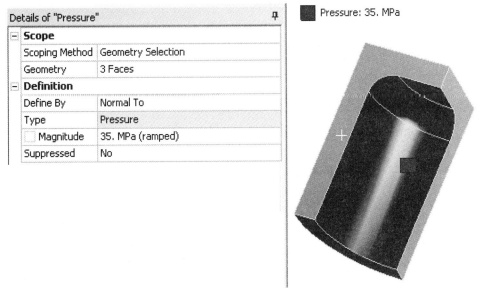

Figure 5-7 Apply pressure loading.

10.   **Solution > Stress > Equivalent (von Mises) Stress**

11.   **Solution >** (Right click) **Solve**

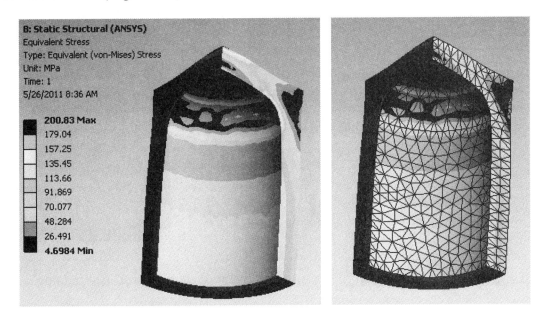

Figure 5-8 Computed von Mises stress using the default mesh.

We compute the von Mises or Equivalent Stress for this problem because the load is static and the steel material is ductile. The von Mises stress is the widely accepted predictor of yielding for cases such as this where a multi-axial state of stress is present. If the **von Mises** stress is greater than or equal to the **material yield stress** (as found in a uniaxial tensile test), yielding, however localized it may be, is predicted. The Equivalent Stress can be computed easily using the principal stresses as shown below.

$$\sigma_e = \sqrt{\frac{(\sigma_1 - \sigma_2)^2 + (\sigma_2 - \sigma_3)^2 + (\sigma_3 - \sigma_1)^2}{2}}$$

We note in the figure above that the stress distribution is not smooth and uniform particularly on the inside corner fillet where the maximum values occur. The problem is symmetric in geometry, material properties, loading, and boundary conditions about the Y axis, so we would expect the solution to be also. We will manually adjust the mesh density to improve the solution.

12.   Mesh > Details of "Mesh" > Advanced > Element Size > 4 mm

Now solve the problem again.

13.   Solution > (Right click) Solve

The new mesh and von Mises stress distribution is shown below. Note that the mesh in most locations has several elements through the 25 mm wall thickness.

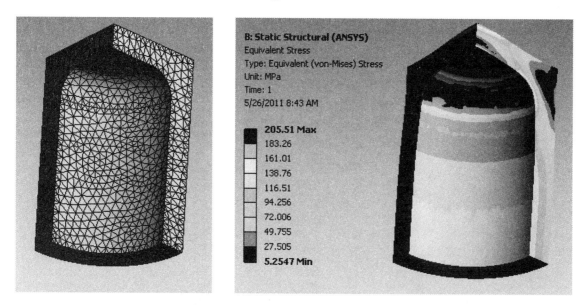

Figure 5-9 Mesh and von Mises stresses for 4 mm element size specification.

These results are not perfect but are much better; we'll accept them and move on. The **Mesh** object in the project tree displays information about the mesh parameters.

14.   Mesh > Statistics

Statistics	
Nodes	15185
Elements	8502
Mesh Metric	None

Figure 5-10 Mesh statistics.

Let's find the stress components at the mid-plane of the complete cylinder (the bottom of our model). Add the normal stresses in the X, Y, and Z directions to the items in the solution object.

15. **Solution > Stress > Normal > Details of "Normal Stress" > Type > Normal Stress > Direction > X Axis**

16. **Repeat for Y and Z axis normal stresses**

17. **Solution > (right click) Evaluate All Results**

18. **Solution > Normal Stress** (X axis) The Sx distribution is shown below. Use the **"123 Probe"** tool to display the X stress at the inside of the cylinder on the face normal to the X axis. 🔳Probe

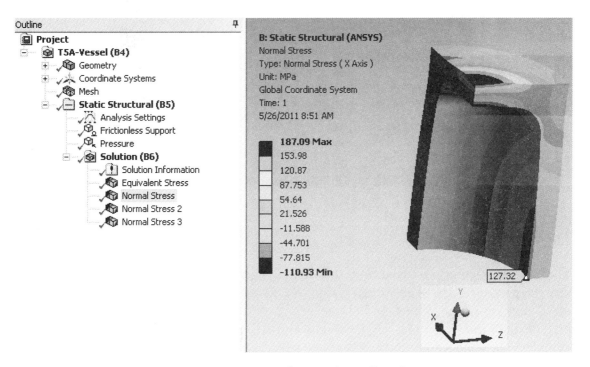

Figure 5-11 Normal stress in X direction.

For the orientation shown, the normal stress in the X direction is what we normally call the cylinder **hoop stress**. The value shown is 127 MPa. Similarly we find the normal stresses in the Y and Z directions at this point to be 46.5 MPa and -34.9 MPa. These correspond to the **axial stress** and the **radial stress** in the cylinder.

Compute the radial deflection also.

19.   Solution > Deformation > Directional > Details of "Directional Deformation" > Type > Directional Deformation > Orientation > Z Axis > Evaluate All Results

The result as shown in the next figure is about 0.0465 mm.

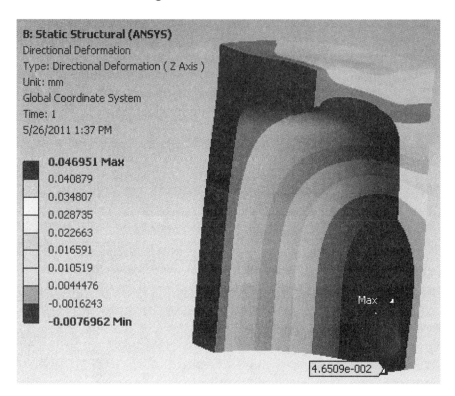

Figure 5-12 Deflection in the Z (radial) direction.

Theoretical Solution

The stresses at points removed from the stress concentration associated with the end caps can be predicted reasonably well using **thick-walled cylinder** equations from solid mechanics or elasticity theory. For the geometry and loading of this example, theory predicts the following radial deflection and stress components at the **inner surface** of the cylinder. The results are summarized in the table below.

Pressure Vessel Results

	Theoretical	Workbench	Error, per cent
Hoop Stress (Sx), MPa	125	127	1.9
Axial Stress (Sy), MPa	45	46.5	3.3
Radial Stress (Sz), MPa	-35	-34.9	0.3
Radial Deflection, mm	0.0458	0.0469	1.5

Thus the Workbench model arrives at a solution within a few per cent of the theoretical values, and, since the theoretical solution assumes a uniform distribution for the axial stress, the Workbench solution may give a better picture of the actual stress state in that instance. Before we quit, let's examine an **alternative meshing**.

In ANSYS Workbench we can manage the mesh in a number of different ways in addition to those already discussed. We illustrate by continuing with an alternate analysis of the pressure vessel.

First clear the results already calculated and return to the basic mesh.

20.   Right click Mesh > Clear Generated Data > Yes

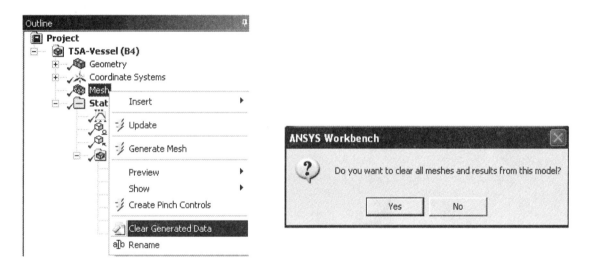

Figure 5-13 Clear results dialog.

21.   Mesh > Details of "Mesh" > Advanced > Element Size > (enter 0, return) Default

22.   Mesh > Relevance Center > Fine > Generate Mesh

Since the interior fillet is the source of stress concentration we will use this geometry to refine the mesh.

23.   **Mesh** > (right click) **Insert** > **Refinement** (Select the interior fillet; see next figure.)

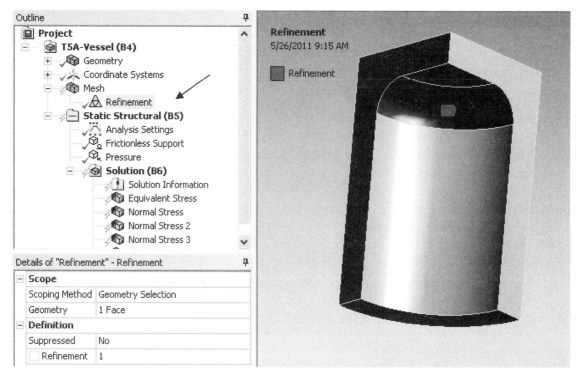

Figure 5-14 Refinement defined by a critical surface.

24.   **Details of Refinement > Geometry > Apply; Refinement 1**

25.   **Mesh > Generate Mesh** (Gives us the following mesh, dense in the high stress area.)

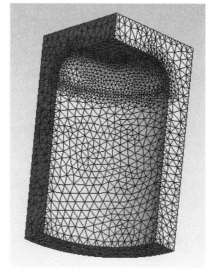

Figure 5-15 Locally refined mesh.

Let's solve this problem and examine the computed results.

26.   Solution > Solve

The von Mises stress distribution is shown next, and we see reasonably smooth contours and computed magnitudes only slightly different from values for the most dense mesh obtained by manual manipulation of the element size specification in the meshing parameters details dialog box.

The **Solution Information** object or **Mesh > Statistics** shows this model to have about **35,000 nodes** and **22,000 elements**.

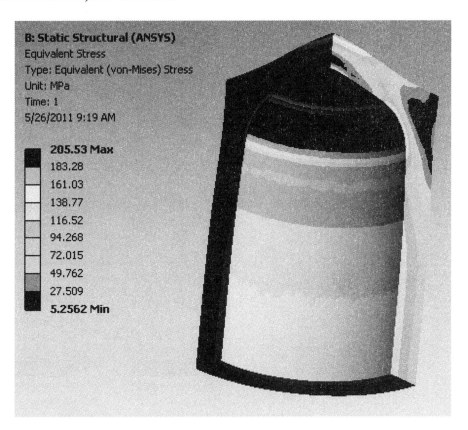

Figure 5-16 Equivalent (von-Mises) Stress.

Another meshing option we have is to insert a convergence object and perform adaptive mesh solutions as discussed in the previous chapter. We leave this as a problem at the end of the chapter.

Because every plane passing through the vertical axis, (Y Fig 5-10) is a plane of symmetry, we can also make this a much smaller problem by creating a model that is just a small wedge, say 10 degrees instead of the 90 degree wedge used above. Try it.

An even smaller, faster solving model is based on a planar, axisymmetric analysis. We will solve the problem that way in Chapter 8.

5-4   TUTORIAL 5B – BRACKET

The **objective** of this tutorial is to compute the **stress** and **deflection** response of the aluminum bracket shown in the figure below. The bracket is10 mm thick, 100 mm tall, 50 mm deep, and 60 mm in width. It has a 30 mm diameter bearing hole located 70 mm from its base plane. The fillet radii are 10 and 20 mm, and the 10 mm mounting bolt holes are located 15 mm from the front and side edges. The bearing is subjected to load components 5500 N in the X direction, 3500 N in Y, and 1700 N in Z. The base of the bracket is fixed against all motion.

The first step is to create the solid model of the bracket. Open ANSYS DesignModeler or other solid modeling system and create the bracket model using the given dimensions.

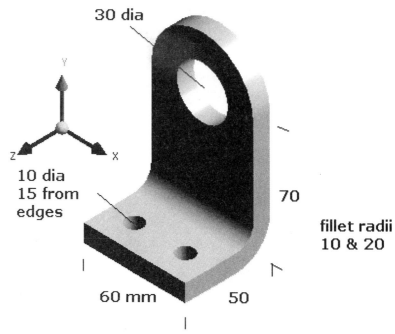

Figure 5-17 Bracket.

1.   Start **ANSYS Workbench,** then **DesignModeler** and **create** or **attach** the **bracket geometry**.

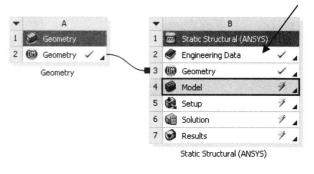

Figure 5-18 T5B Project Schematic.

We will use the aluminum properties from the ANSYS library for the analysis. Add **Aluminum Alloy** to the **Engineering Data**.

Double Click cell B2, Engineering Data

Be sure **View > Properties & Outline** and **Engineering Data Sources** are turned on.

2.   **Select General Materials > Aluminum Alloy > Click** ⊞ **to add this material to the project.**

Figure 5-19 Aluminum Alloy material properties.

Select **Return to Project**   ⟵ Return to Project   (Top of screen)

3.   **Right Click Model > Refresh**

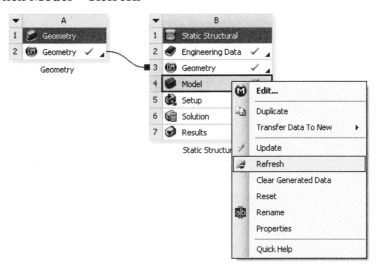

Figure 5-20 Refresh Model.

M **Mechanical > Lbrack > Material > Aluminum Alloy**

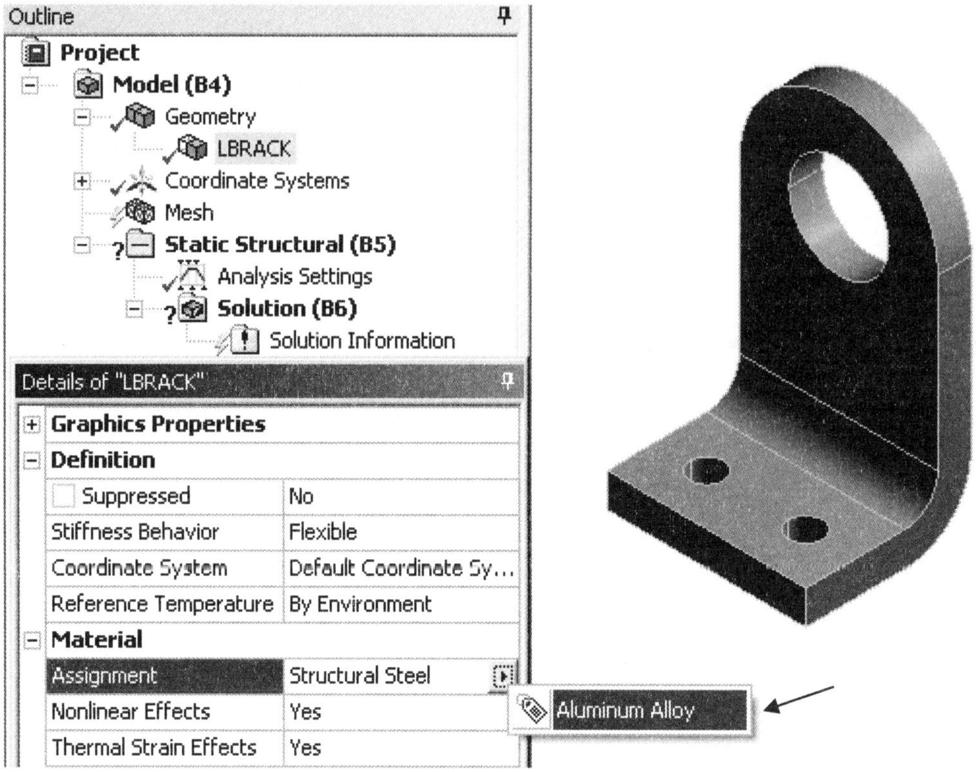

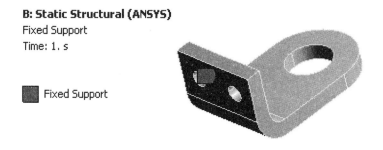

Figure 5-21 Select aluminum alloy.

4.   **Environment > Supports > Fixed Support >** Select the **bottom > Apply**

B: Static Structural (ANSYS)
Fixed Support
Time: 1. s

■   Fixed Support

Figure 5-22 Fixed support.

The **Bearing Load** object does not allow an axial component, so the load conditions are applied to the bearing surface as a **Force** load. Use **Ctrl** to select multiple segments of the bore surface if need be.

5.   **Environment > Loads > Force >** Select the **bearing surface(s) > Apply**

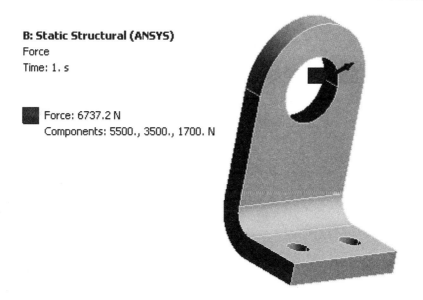

Figure 5-23 Applied load.

Add **Equivalent Stress**, **Total Deformation**, and **Structural Error** to the items to be computed.

6. **Solution > Stress > Equivalent (von Mises)**

7. **Solution > Deformation > Total**

8. **Solution > Stress > Error**

9. **Solve**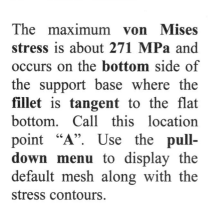

The maximum **von Mises stress** is about **271 MPa** and occurs on the **bottom** side of the support base where the **fillet** is **tangent** to the flat bottom. Call this location point "**A**". Use the **pull-down menu** to display the default mesh along with the stress contours.

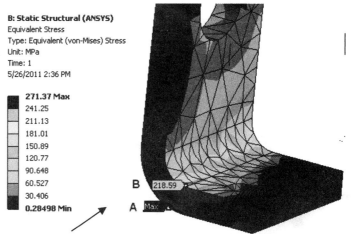

Figure 5-24 von Mises stress distribution.

The maximum von Mises stress on the **top surface** of the bracket is about **219 MPa** and is located near point "**B**" as shown.

The **total deformation** (vector sum of components) is shown next, and it's no surprise that the maximum value is at the top of the bracket. Its value is about **1.3 mm**.

Next we plot the **estimated error** and find that the maximum value is on the bottom of the bracket where the fixed support surface ends at the tangent point of the fillet radius with the fixed bottom surface. The estimated error ranges from around 2e-3 to 25 mJ and indicates a singularity where the fixed support surface abruptly ends much like a **zero radius interior corner**.

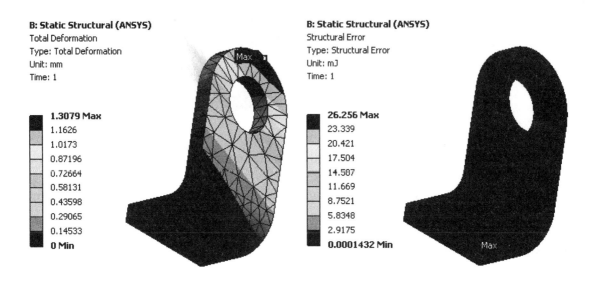

Figure 5-25 Total deformation and error estimate.

If we set the element size to 2.5 mm under Details of "Mesh" (almost 7,000 elements) and solve the problem again, the computed total deflection increases to about 1.36 mm. The von Mises stress at point **B** on top increases to **230 MPa** and stress on the bottom at the singular point **A** increases to **352 MPa**.

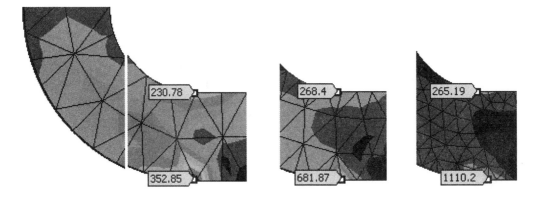

Figure 5-26 Equivalent stress for three different mesh sizes.

If we reduce the characteristic element size again, the maximum deflection remains the same but the singular stress continues to change (**681 MPa**). The stress at point B remains essentially constant. (Your ability to solve problems with a large number of elements will depend upon the capability of the computer hardware you are using.)

Reduce the characteristic element size even further to 1.0 mm; the singular stress increases to **1110 MPa** but the stress at point **A** is about **265 MPa**.

Interpretation of the stress at point A depends, among other things, upon support details, characteristic of the load (static or dynamic), material (brittle or ductile; this example assumes a ductile aluminum). In the actual part, the contact area between the bottom and its support may increase or decrease as bending of the bracket occurs. We see that determination of appropriate loadings and boundary conditions can be much more difficult than modeling the geometry.

5-5 TUTORIAL 5C – CLEVIS ASSEMBLY

In the final tutorial of this chapter we examine the stress and deformations in the clevis component of the yoke-stem-pin assembly discussed at the end of Chapter 2. The **objective** is to determine the **yoke stresses** caused by a **tensile load** carried by the yoke and stem.

1.   Start **ANSYS Workbench** and **DesignModeler; attach the yoke assembly**. The assembly can be developed in ANSYS DesignModeler or in another solid modeler of your choice. See T2C in Chapter 2 for dimensions.

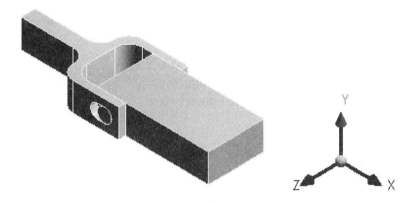

Figure 5-27 Clevis, pin, stem model.

2.   **Check the units settings** to be sure you're using **in-lbf-sec**.

3.   **Expand** the **Geometry** object in the simulation outline tree.

There are **three solids** in the geometry item: the **Yoke**, the **Stem**, and the **Pin**. If need be, **right click on the label "Solid"** and **rename** the items yoke, stem or pin. We accept the default **structural steel material** for all the parts.

4.   Expand the **Contact** object in the simulation outline tree.

There are **three regions of contact** in the assembly: the **insides of the yoke fingers contacting the sides of the stem**, the **pin contacting the hole in the stem**, and the **pin contacting the slots in the yoke fingers**.

5.   Click on each of the three contact items in turn. We see the three different contact surfaces as shown below. The order of your contact surfaces may be different depending upon how you built your assembly model.

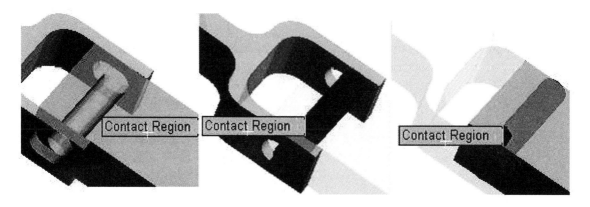

Figure 5-28 Three contact surfaces.

There are a number of different contact models available to us to represent different kinds of contacting surfaces. Click on the first contact item and examine the options.

6.   Contact > Contact Region > Details of "Contact Region" > Definition > Type

The options for the type of contact are: **Bonded**, **No Separation**, **Frictionless**, **Rough**, and **Frictional**. The **default** selection is **Bonded**.

Figure 5-29 Types of contact modeling available.

These contact types are defined as follows: (From the **ANSYS Mechanical Help** files. Search on

Details of "Contact Region"	坪
Scope	
Scoping Method	Geometry Selection
Contact	2 Faces
Target	2 Faces
Contact Bodies	
Target Bodies	
Definition	
Type	Bonded
Scope Mode	Bonded
Behavior	No Separation / Frictionless
Suppressed	Rough
Advanced	Frictional
Formulation	Pure Penalty
Normal Stiffness	Program Controlled
Update Stiffness	Never
Thermal Conductance	Program Controlled
Pinball Region	Program Controlled

'Contact' then select information on the 'Type' of contact.):

- **"Type**: The differences in the contact settings determine how the contacting bodies can move relative to one another. This is the most common setting and has the most impact on what other settings are available. Most of these types only apply to contact regions made up of faces only.

  - **Bonded**: This is the default configuration for contact regions. If contact regions are bonded, then no sliding or separation between faces or edges is allowed. Think of the region as *glued*. This type of contact allows for a linear solution since the contact length/area will not change during the application of the load. If contact is determined on the mathematical model, any gaps will be closed and any initial penetration will be ignored.
  - **No Separation**: This contact setting is similar to the bonded case. It only applies to regions of faces. Separation of faces in contact is not allowed, but small amounts of frictionless sliding can occur along contact faces.
  - **Frictionless**: This setting models standard unilateral contact; that is, normal pressure equals zero if separation occurs. It only applies to regions of faces. Thus gaps can form in the model between bodies depending on the loading. This solution is nonlinear because the area of contact may change as the load is applied. A zero coefficient of friction is assumed, thus allowing free sliding. The model should be well constrained when using this contact setting. Weak springs are added to the assembly to help stabilize the model in order to achieve a reasonable solution.
  - **Rough**: Similar to the frictionless setting, this setting models perfectly rough frictional contact where there is no sliding. It only applies to regions of faces. By default, no automatic closing of gaps is performed. This case corresponds to an infinite friction coefficient between the contacting bodies.
  - **Frictional**: In this setting, two contacting faces can carry shear stresses up to a certain magnitude across their interface before they start sliding relative to each other. It only applies to regions of faces. This state is known as "sticking." The model defines an equivalent shear stress at which sliding on the face begins as a fraction of the contact pressure. Once the shear stress is exceeded, the two faces will slide relative to each other. The coefficient of friction can be any non-negative value.

Choosing the appropriate contact type depends on the type of problem you are trying to solve. If modeling the ability of bodies to separate or open slightly is important and/or obtaining the stresses very near a contact interface is important, consider using one of the nonlinear contact types (**Frictionless**, **Rough**, **Frictional**), which can model gaps and more accurately model the true area of contact. However, using these contact types usually results in longer solution times and can have possible convergence problems due to the contact nonlinearity. If convergence problems arise or if determining the exact area of contact is critical, consider using a finer mesh (using the Sizing control) on the contact faces or edges."

We will focus in our example on the **pin contacting the slots in the yoke fingers** and the **stress in the yoke**. If we assume that the pin is tightly fit into the hole in the stem, **Bonded** is an appropriate choice for this contacting pair. As deformation occurs, the yoke fingers bend outward and may loose contact with the sides of the stem. We will use a **Frictional** model for this contact as well as the contact between the pin and the yoke. For these two a friction coefficient of **0.2** between the two steel surfaces is assumed.

7. **Set the contact types** to **Frictional, Bonded, Frictional.** (Your order may be different.)

8. **Apply a -1000 psi** (a negative pressure) to the **Stem** also in the **X Direction.** The stem cross sectional area is 2 sq. inches, so this corresponds to a **tensile load of 2,000 lbf. Restrict the Yoke** from motion in the **X Direction.**

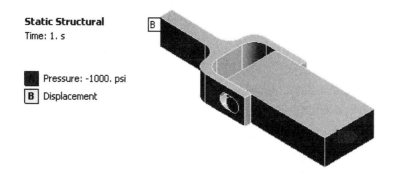

Figure 5-30 Structural environment conditions.

9. **Select X Direction Displacement, X Direction Normal Stress** and **Equivalent Stress** as the solution items.

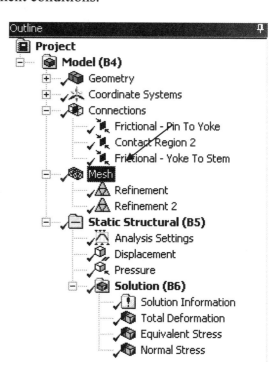

Figure 5-31 Project Outline.

Create a medium default mesh.

10. **Mesh > Details of Mesh > Sizing > Medium > Generate Mesh**

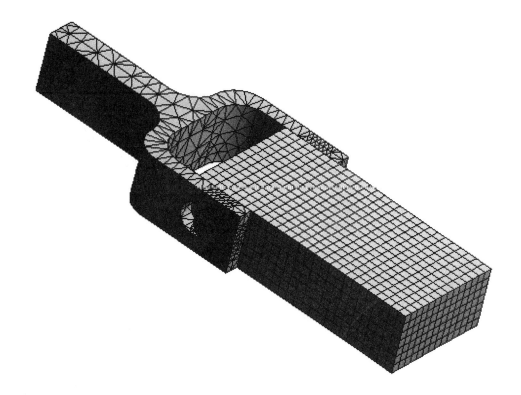

Figure 5-32 Default medium mesh.

We will **refine the default mesh** at the pin-yoke contact surfaces in order to increase the accuracy of the modeling in this region.

To isolate the yoke so we can see the contact surface, hide the other objects.

11.   **Geometry > Right Click Yoke > Hide All Other Bodies**

Figure 5-33 Isolate the yoke.

12.   **Right Click Mesh > Insert > Refinement**

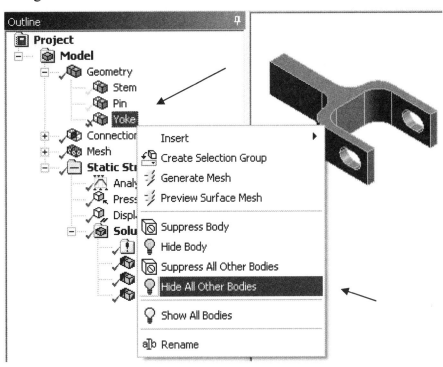

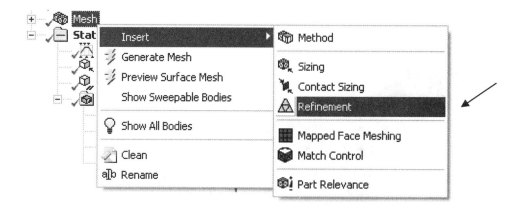

Figure 5-34 Insert refinement.

13.   Use Ctrl Select to select the yoke slot surfaces.

14.   Repeat this process to isolate the pin and **refine its surface.**

The refined meshes are shown below.

Show all the bodies and then **solve** the simulation model.

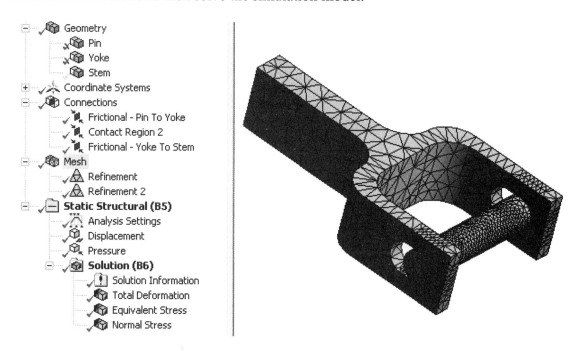

Figure 5-35 Yoke and pin mesh refinements.

15.   Solve ⤳ Solve

Rigid body motions are not completely restrained by the boundary conditions, so the **Weak Springs Added Warning** message is displayed. The following figure shows the computed von Mises stresses with a maximum over **27 kpsi**.

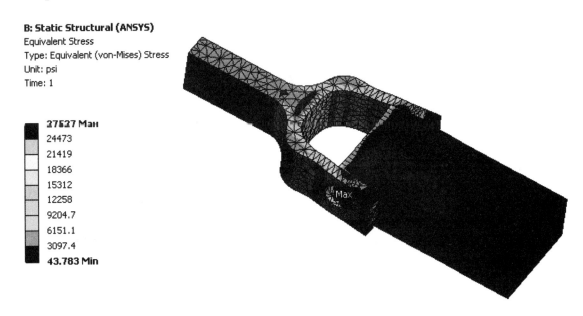

B: Static Structural (ANSYS)
Equivalent Stress
Type: Equivalent (von-Mises) Stress
Unit: psi
Time: 1

27527 Max
24473
21419
18366
15312
12258
9204.7
6151.1
3097.4
43.783 Min

Figure 5-36 Computed von Mises stress.

Hide all bodies except the yoke and display the computed stresses in the yoke.

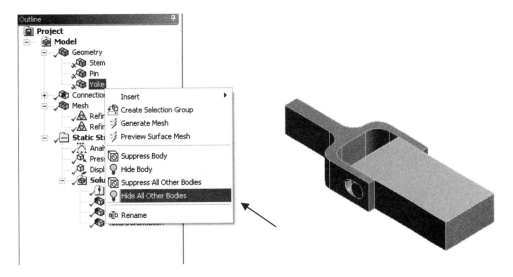

Figure 5-37 Isolate the yoke for evaluation.

The figure below shows the yoke von Mises and X Direction normal stress distributions in the yoke. The maximum values occur in the thin region of the yoke slots.

Figure 5-38 Stresses in the yoke.

Be sure to animate the deformation in order to aid your understanding of the model you have created. You may notice small rigid body type motions.

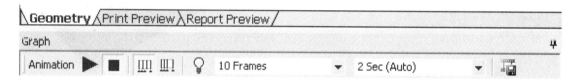

Figure 5-39 Animation menu.

Symmetry can be used to eliminate all rigid body motions and avoid the automatic addition of weak springs to ground to stabilize the model. To enforce symmetric behavior, open the clevis assembly in the solid modeler and remove three quarters of the solid model, say the bottom and right portions as shown in the figure below.

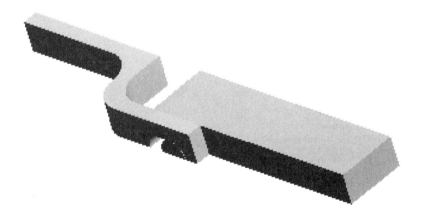

Figure 5-40 Quadrant of clevis assembly

Apply displacement boundary conditions that prevent motion of the exposed planes of symmetry surface in directions perpendicular to those surfaces.

5-6 SUMMARY

The tutorials of Chapter 5 illustrate the use of ANSYS Mechanical for calculation of stress and deflection response of typical three-dimensional solids. Included is an example of analysis of an assembly with contacting parts. In the next chapter we examine the many wizards and tools provided by ANSYS Mechanical to assist with simulations of the type described in this book.

5-7 PROBLEMS

5-1 Determine the magnitude and location of the **maximum von Mises** stress for the cylinder of Tutorial 5A if the 35 MPa pressure is an **external pressure**.

5-2 The structural steel "Z" bracket shown below is 5 inches wide with 0.5 inch radius rounds. Remove the hole that is shown and find the maximum downward **displacement** and maximum **von Mises stress at A**, the midpoint of the sloping section.

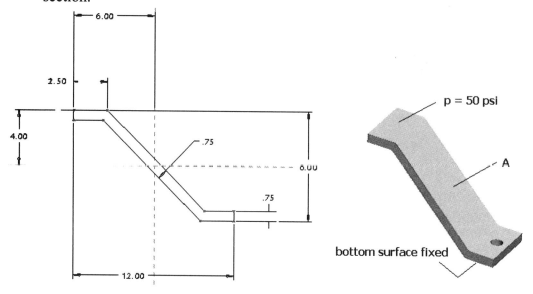

Figure P5-2

5-3 The structural steel shaft below is fixed at the left end and free on the right. Find the free end **deflection** and **von Mises stress** at the 7.5 mm radius step if the applied load is **400 kN**.

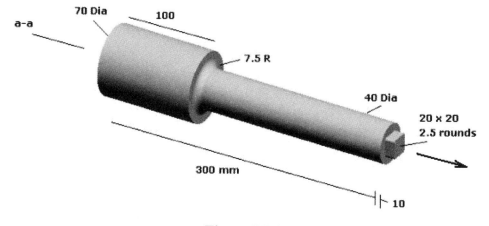

Figure P5-3

5-4   Repeat Problem 5-3 but with the end load applied vertically so as to put the shaft in bending.

5-5   The flat head of the cylinder of Tutorial 5A is replaced with a head that is hemispherical. Find the magnitude and location of the **maximum principal tensile stress** due the 35 MPa internal pressure if the cylinder is made of gray cast iron. Report your computed stress results in MPa and in psi. Also find the maximum outward deflection of a point on the inner surface.

5-6   The structural steel anchor device is loaded by an axial force as shown. All of the lower surfaces are fixed as indicated. Note that the center of the 5 mm Diameter groove is aligned with the outer surfaces of the anchor as shown in the sketch. Find the magnitude and location of the **maximum principal stress** and the **maximum deflection**.

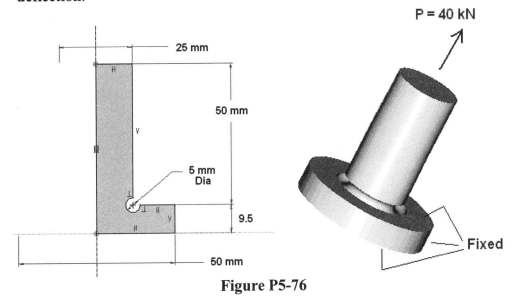

Figure P5-76

5-7   Repeat Problem 5-6 but with the end load applied horizontally so as to put the anchor in bending.

5-8   Select your own dimensions and material, create a solid model of a foot control lever such as the one shown in the figure below, and determine the magnitude and location of the maximum **von Mises stress** and the maximum downward **deflection** if a load equal to your weight is applied to the foot plate while the inside of the cylindrical bore is held fixed in all directions.

Figure P5-8

NOTES:

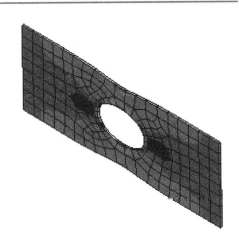

Chapter 6

Wizards & Tools

6-1 OVERVIEW

ANSYS Mechanical provides a number of Tools and Wizards to assist with successful simulation projects. This Chapter illustrates the use of these typical applications. In particular we discuss the use of

- ♦ Wizards for simulation problem setup

- ♦ Tools for simulation assessment

6-2 INTRODUCTION

ANSYS Mechanical provides a large number of aids and help file information to assist the user with problem setup and interpretation of computed results. In this chapter we discuss their use for problems involving static loading and fatigue loading. Wizards and tools for other problem types are covered in later discussions.

6-3 TUTORIAL 6A – STATIC LOADINGS - DUCTILE MATERIALS

In this tutorial we compute the stress state and deflection response of the plate with a central hole that was considered at the beginning of Chapter 4 but use an ANSYS Mechanical Wizard to assist with the solution. The **1000 x 400 x 10 mm** plate is shown in the illustration below. It has a central circular hole **200 mm** in **diamete**r and supports an axial **tensile load** of **100 kN**.

Figure 6-1 Plate with central hole.

The first step is to create the **solid model** of the bracket. Open ANSYS DesignModeler or another parametric modeling system, develop the solid model of the **complete plate** and save it for use later.

1.   **Start ANSYS Workbench** and **attach the plate geometry. Start Mechanical**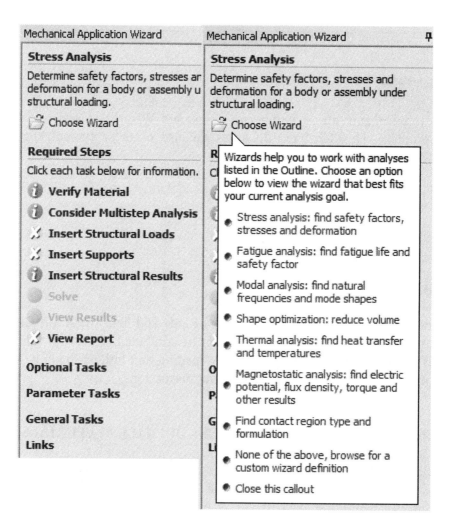

2.   If the **Mechanical Application Wizard** is not shown on the right hand edge of the screen, select the **green check** icon, top menu 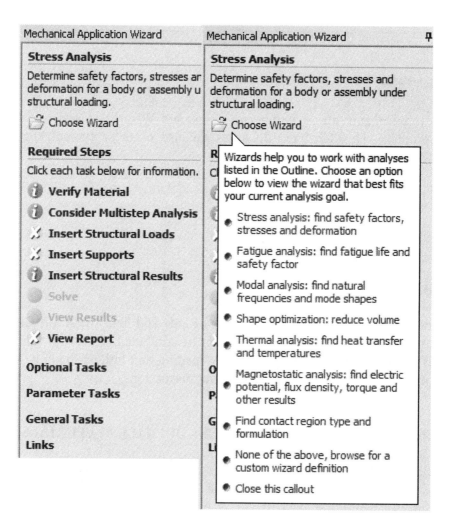.

The Wizard Menus outline the steps to be taken in a Mechanical Application.

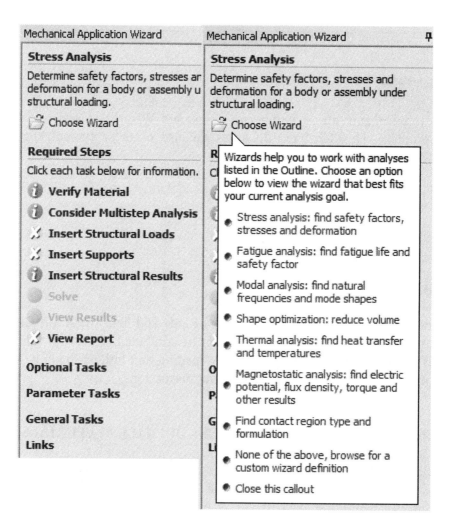

Figure 6-2 Simulation Wizard menus.

3.   Select **Choose Wizard** to view the **seven predefined wizards** available to you. **Stress Analysis** is the **default.** Then **Close this callout**.

In the Stress Analysis Wizard an 'X' indicates a step that has not been completed while a Check marks a completed step. Additional information is indicated with an 'i' .

4.   Verify Material

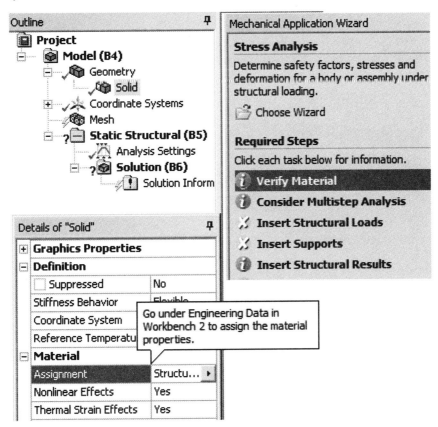

Figure 6-3 Verify the material assigned to this part.

5.   Double click cell B2 – Engineering Data in the **Workbench 2 Project Schematic** to review the material properties.

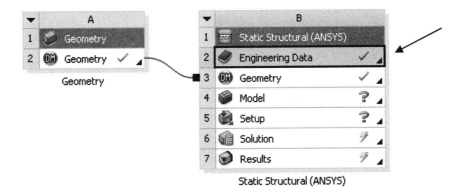

Figure 6-4 Workbench 2 Project Schematic.

Be sure **View** > **Properties & Outline** and **Engineering Data Sources** are turned on.

6.   **Select General Materials > Structural Steel**

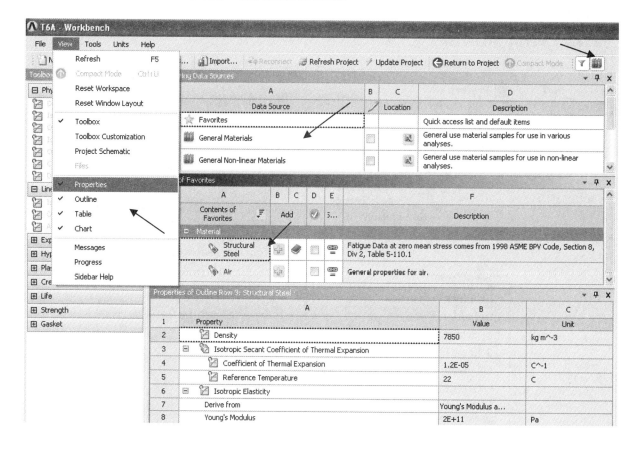

Figure 6-5 Material properties.

We will not change any of these quantities but note the values of the **Yield** and **Ultimate Strengths** for the default structural steel. **Return** to **Project** (top of screen).

7.   **Return** to **Mechanical**

The next item on the list of **Required Steps** is **Consider Multistep Analysis**.

Figure 6-6 Multistep Loads information.

Our load is applied in **one step**.

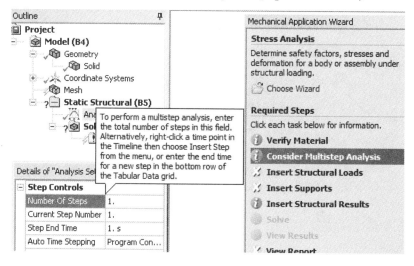

8.   **Insert Structural Loads**

Apply a **force of 100 kN** in the **x direction** to the **right end face** of the plate and a **force of -100 kN** in the **x direction** to the **left** end.

9.   **Environment > Loads > Force > Click** right end surface.

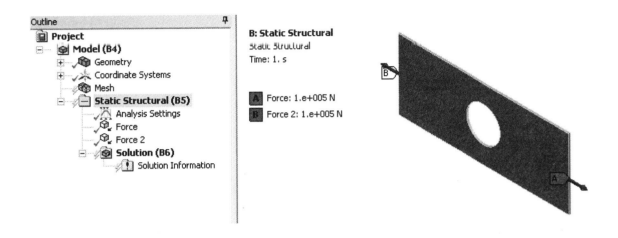

Figure 6-7 Apply loads loading.

10.   **Details of "Force" > Geometry > Apply**

11.   **Details of "Force" > Magnitude > 100,000**

On the left > Magnitude > -100,000

Insert Loads is now checked off, and the next item is **Insert Supports**. We are not going to supply any supports and see if the **Weak Springs** feature will take care of the rigid body motion well enough.

Required Steps
Click each task below for information.
- ⓘ **Verify Material**
- ⓘ **Consider Multistep Analysis**
- ✓ **Insert Structural Loads**
- ✗ **Insert Supports**
- ⓘ **Insert Structural Results**
- ⚡ **Solve**
- ◯ **View Results**
- ⚡ **View Report**

Figure 6-8 Wizard status.

12.   **Insert Structural Results** is the next item in the wizard.

13.   **Solution > Stress > Equivalent Stress**

14.   **Solution > Deformation > Total Deformation**

15.   **Solution > Tools > Stress Tool**

16.   **Solution > Tools > Stress Tool > Safety Margin**

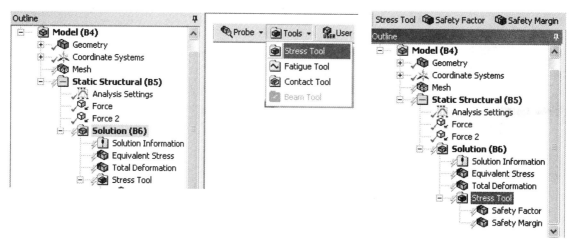

Figure 6-9 Insert structural results and analysis Tools.

17.   Solve

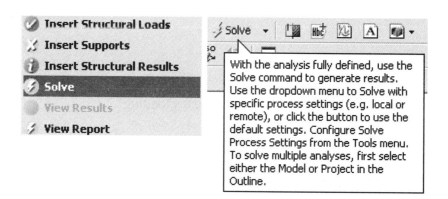

Figure 6-10 'Solve' information message.

We get the solution status message and the rigid-body warning message as shown below.

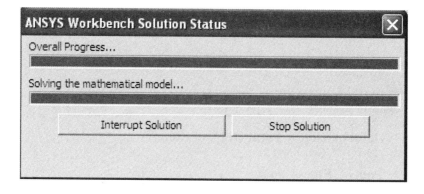

Figure 6-11 Solution status.

This model has no displacement constraints to prevent rigid body motion from occurring. To suppress **rigid body motion**, ANSYS Workbench automatically adds **weak spring supports** and issues a warning in the message box at the bottom of the screen.

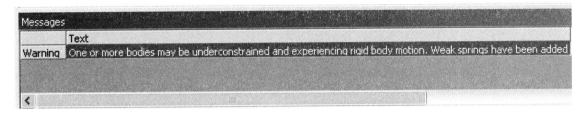

Figure 6-12 Rigid body motion warning.

The Wizard menu is complete and we are ready to **View Results**.

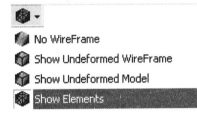

18. **Solution > Equivalent Stress**

19. **Edges > Show Elements**

Figure 6-13 Show the mesh.

Results from the default mesh are a little ragged, so create a relevance center **fine mesh**.

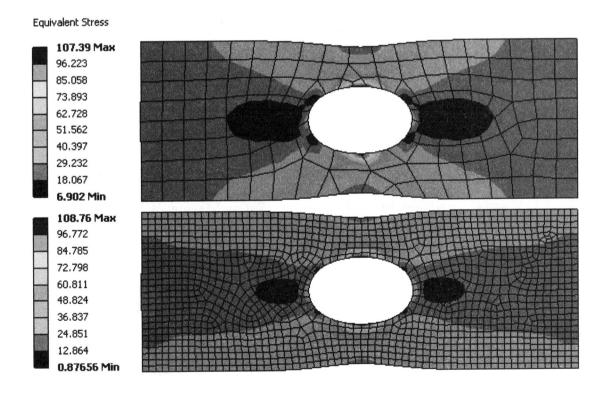

Figure 6-14 von Mises stress distribution.

For ductile materials under static loading, yielding may be predicted by comparing the **Maximum Equivalent Stress (von Mises Stress)** in the part with the **Tensile Yield Strength** observed during testing of a tensile sample of the part material when the tensile sample yielded. The **Equivalent Stress** method is generally considered the most appropriate approach for ductile materials under static loading.

The **Equivalent Stress** or **von Mises Stress** is based on the observation that the hydrostatic component of a general stress state does not influence yielding in a ductile material and it combines the various stresses in a complex multi-axis component stress situation into a single quantity as follows:

$$\sigma_e = \sqrt{\frac{(\sigma_1 - \sigma_2)^2 + (\sigma_2 - \sigma_3)^2 + (\sigma_3 - \sigma_1)^2}{2}}$$

The stress tool wizard automatically inserts the **Safety Factor** computation and we added the **Safety Margin**. If S_y is the material **Yield Strength**, the **Factor of Safety** and the **Margin of Safety** are defined as:

$$F_s = \frac{S_y}{\sigma_e} \qquad\qquad M_s = F_s - 1$$

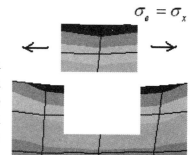

$$\sigma_e = \sigma_x$$

In T4A we calculated the Max stress in the X-direction, Sx and found a value of 109 MPa. For this simple problem Sx max occurs in the X-direction at the surface of the hole, so the von Mises and Normal Stress in X direction are equal in this problem since the stresses in the Y and Z directions are zero.

Figure 6-15 Max Stress.

For this problem the maximum von Mises stress is **109 MPa** and the material yield stress is **250 MPa**. We can easily use the computed stress (109) and the yield strength (250) to compute the factor of safety by hand. **Fs = 250/109 = 2.3**.

20. **Click Stress Tool**, then **Safety Factor**, then **Safety Margin**. We see the following in the details boxes. Minimum values of these are the significant quantities.

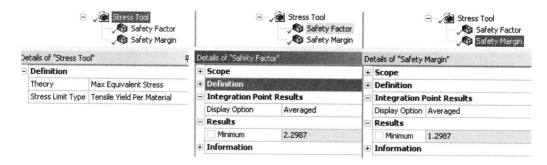

Figure 6-16 Stress tool results.

Check to see if the lack of constraints caused any undesirable rigid body motion.

21. Solution > Total Deformation > Animation > Play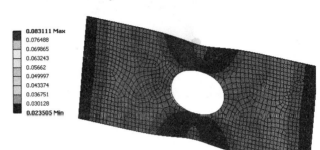

Figure 6-17 Deformation plot.

Use the movie icon ⬛ to capture the animation in an **AVI file**.

The animation indicates that the automatic imposition of weak springs solved the rigid body motion issue adequately. To check further, insert Y and Z direction displacements in the solution and note that the slight rigid body displacement in the Z direction is of little consequence. If you wish, use a quadrant model with appropriate boundary conditions as in Chapter 4 to prevent any spurious rigid body motion.

The only item left on the wizard list of required steps is **View Report**. Before viewing the report, **insert a figure** of the **Equivalent Stress Distribution** in the solution. This figure will appear in the report.

22. Solution > Equivalent Stress. New Figure or Image (Select the top row icon)

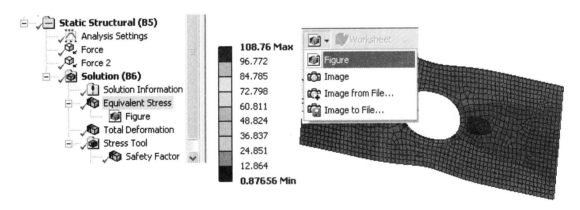

Figure 6-18 Insert a figure.

Now select view report. A portion of the report is shown below.

23. Simulation Wizard > View Report (or **Report Preview** lower tab)

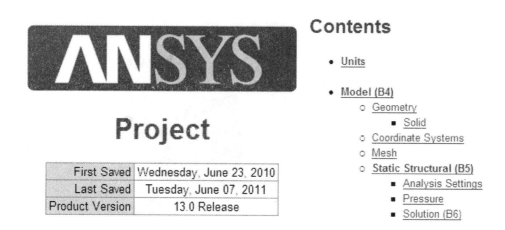

Figure 6-19 Report first page and partial contents.

The details of the project are included in this report including any figures that were inserted in the solution. Once the report has been generated, it can be printed, published, sent as an email, imported into Word or Power Point, or refreshed as project tree items change by selecting from the icon menu below.

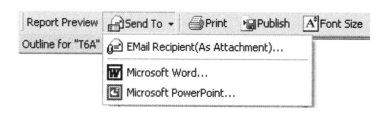

Figure 6-20 Report options.

24.   Save your work as T6A.

The results of this tutorial show that the maximum equivalent or von Mises stress computed for this loading and geometry is around **109 MPa**, and based upon the **equivalent stress method** and a material **tensile yield strength** of **250 MPa**, the predicted **factor of safety** for the part is around **2.3**. You may wish to insert an error estimate, refine the mesh, and evaluate these measures again, but we leave that for a problem. In the next tutorial we will solve the same problem but assume that the part is made of a brittle material.

6-4   TUTORIAL 6B – STATIC LOADINGS – BRITTLE MATERIALS

Two changes to the analysis are required to consider the plate with a central hole to be made of a **brittle material (Gray Cast Iron)**. We need to change the material specification as well as the solution quantities and the details of the factor and margin of safety. Use the same geometry and loading for this tutorial as in Tutorial 6A.

1.   **Verify Material**

2.   Return to **Workbench** > Double click **cell B2 Engineering Data**
Be sure **View** > **Properties & Outline** and **Engineering Data Sources** are turned on.

[Engineering Data Sources]   (top of screen)

3.   **General Materials > Gray Cast Iron**

Outline Filter				
▼	A	B	C	D
1	Data Source	✎	Location	Description
2	Engineering Data		B2	Contents filtered for Static Structural (ANSYS).
3	General Materials	☐	☒	General use material samples for use in various analyses.
4	General Non-linear Materials	☐	☒	General use material samples for use in non-linear analyses.
5	Explicit Materials	☐	☒	Material samples for use in an explicit anaylsis.
6	Hyperelastic Materials	☐	☒	Material stress-strain data samples for curve fitting.
7	Magnetic B-H Curves	☐	☒	B-H Curve samples specific for use in a magnetic analysis.

Outline of General Materials					
▼	A	B	C	D	E
1	Contents of General Materials	Add	S..		Description
5	Concrete	✚		🔗	
6	Copper Alloy	✚		🔗	
7	Gray Cast Iron	✚		🔗	
8	Magnesium Alloy	✚		🔗	

Properties of Outline Row 7: Gray Cast Iron			
▼	A	B	C
1	Property	Value	Unit
2	Density	7200	kg m^-3
3	⊟ Isotropic Secant Coefficient of Thermal Expansion		
4	Coefficient of Thermal Expansion	1.1E-05	C^-1
5	Reference Temperature	22	C
6	⊟ Isotropic Elasticity		
7	Derive from	Young's M.	
8	Young's Modulus	1.1E+11	Pa
9	Poisson's Ratio	0.28	
10	Bulk Modulus	8.3333E+10	Pa
11	Shear Modulus	4.2969E+10	Pa
12	Tensile Yield Strength	0	Pa
13	Compressive Yield Strength	0	Pa
14	Tensile Ultimate Strength	2.4E+08	Pa
15	Compressive Ultimate Strength	8.2E+08	Pa

Figure 6-21 Material properties for gray cast iron.

Particularly note the values of **yield** and **ultimate strength** for gray cast iron.

4.   **Select the + sign to add gray cast iron to the engineering data. > Return to Project** ⊙ Return to Project

5.   **Refresh the Model** to make this material available to the part.

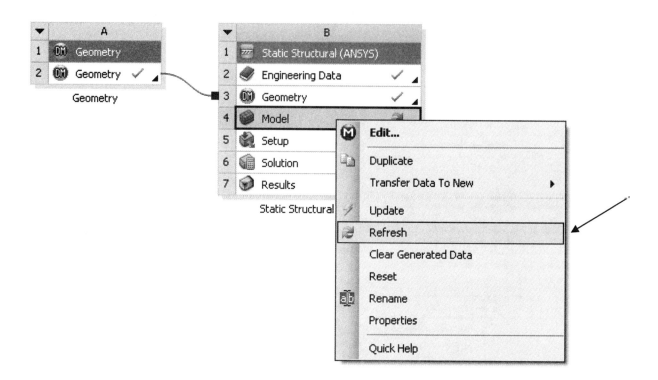

Figure 6-22 Refresh the Model.

6.   **Return** to **Mechanical > Change** from **Structural Steel** to **Gray Cast Iron.**

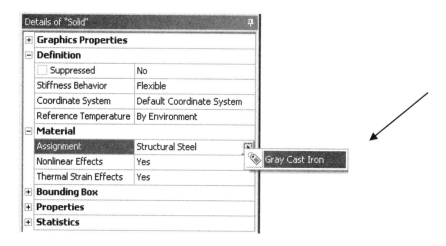

Figure 6-23 Change from Structural Steel to Gray Cast Iron.

7.   **Delete** the **Equivalent Stress** object from the **outline tree.**

Add the maximum and minimum principal stress objects to the outline.

8.   **Solution > Stress > Maximum Principal**

9.   **Solution > Stress > Minimum Principal**

Change the stress tool theory from **Max Equivalent** to **Mohr-Coulomb Stress**

10.   **Solution > Stress Tool > Mohr-Coulomb Stress**

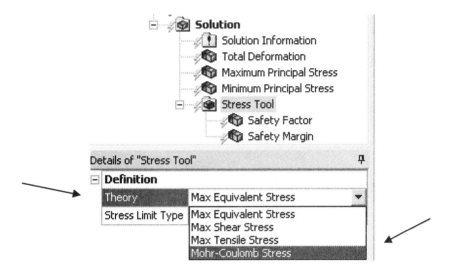

Figure 6-24 Project tree.

Make sure the **Limit Types** are the material **Ultimate Strengths.**

11.   **Solution > Stress Tool > Tensile Limit Type > Tensile Ultimate Per Material**

12.   **Solution > Stress Tool > Compressive Limit Type > Compressive Ultimate Per Material**

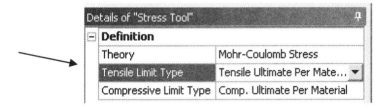

Figure 6-25 Details of Stress Tool.

The Mohr-Coulomb method may be used to predict failure of parts made from brittle materials. The Mohr-Coulomb method takes into account the differences between tensile ultimate strength and compressive ultimate strength that are common in brittle materials (**240 MPa** and **820 MPa** in this case). The method compares the maximum principal tensile stress σ_1 to the material ultimate tensile strength S_{ut} and the minimum principal stress σ_3 with the material ultimate compressive strength S_{uc}. No fracture is predicted if

$$\frac{\sigma_1}{S_{ut}} + \frac{\sigma_3}{S_{uc}} < 1$$ σ_1 and σ_3 must be evaluated at the same point in the past.

The factor of safety and margin of safety are defined as

$$\frac{1}{F_s} = \frac{\sigma_1}{S_{ut}} + \frac{\sigma_3}{S_{uc}} \qquad\qquad M_s = F_s - 1$$

All of the required steps in the simulation wizard are now complete and we can solve for the response.

13. Solve ⫸ Solve

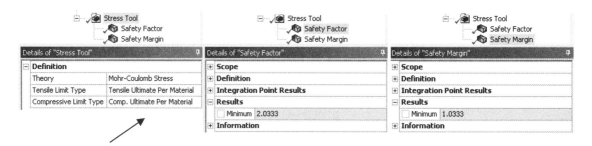

Figure 6-26 Stress Tool Results.

The minimum **factor of safety** based upon the **Mohr-Coulomb** (or Coulomb-Mohr) method is found to be **2.2** giving a **1.2** or **120 per cent margin of safety**. The figure below shows the distribution of the computed results for safety factor.

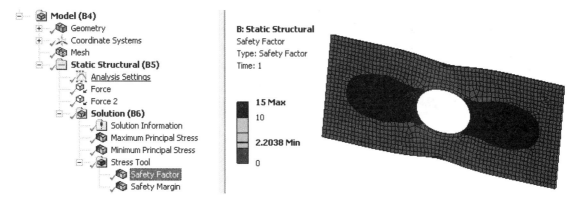

Figure 6-27 Computed safety factor.

In this problem $\sigma_3 = 0$ at the point where $\sigma_1 = $ a maximum $= 109$ MPa, Coulomb-Mohr reduces to the maximum normal stress theory $F_s = S_{ut} / \sigma_{1max} = 240/109 = 2.2$

14.   Save your work as T6B.

In the next section we consider the use of simulation wizard for **fatigue analysis**.

6-5   TUTORIAL 6C – FATIGUE LOADINGS – DUCTILE MATERIALS

Return to the problem of Tutorial 6A but now consider a fatigue environment for the **ductile steel plate**.

1.   Start ANSYS Workbench; Open T6A, and turn on **Simulation Wizard.**

2.   From Choose Wizard Select Fatigue (See the figure below.)

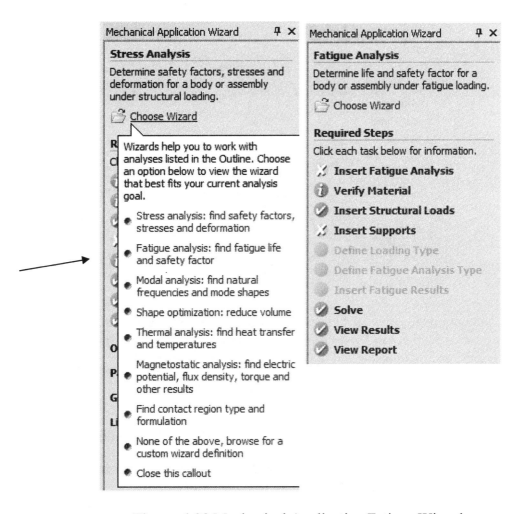

Figure 6-28 Mechanical Application Fatigue Wizard.

3.   **Insert Fatigue Analysis**   

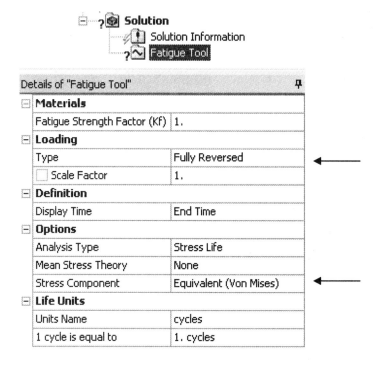

Figure 6-29 Fatigue simulation wizard.

Figure 6-30 Fatigue tool details.

Select the default options to consider the case of a **completely reversed loading** based on a **stress S-N curve** using the **von Mises equivalent stress** method to combine stress with no surface, size, etc. corrections applied to the material properties ($K_f = 1$).

4.   **Solution > Stress > Equivalent Stress**

Use the **default structural steel** for the material. Reset the part material if necessary.

5.   **Verify Material > Return to Workbench > Double Click B2 – Engineering Data**

6.   **Verify Fatigue Data**   *Verify Fatigue Data*

Outline of Schematic B2: Engineering Data

	A	B	C	D
1	Contents of Engineering Data		S..	Description
5	Gray Cast Iron 3	☐		
6	Structural Steel	☐		Fatigue Data at zero mean stress comes from 1998 ASME BPV Code, Section 8, Div 2, Table 5-110.1

Properties of Outline Row 6: Structural Steel

	A	B	C	D	E
1	Property	Value	Unit		
2	Density	7850	kg m^-3	☐	☐
3	⊟ Isotropic Secant Coefficient of Thermal Expansion			☐	
4	Coefficient of Thermal Expansion	1.2E-05	C^-1		☐
5	Reference Temperature	22	C		☐
6	⊟ Isotropic Elasticity			☐	
7	Derive from	Young's M.			
8	Young's Modulus	2E+11	Pa		☐
9	Poisson's Ratio	0.3			☐
10	Bulk Modulus	1.6667E+11	Pa		☐
11	Shear Modulus	7.6923E+10	Pa		☐
12	⊟ Alternating Stress Mean Stress	Tabular		☐	

Figure 6-31 Structural steel material data.

7. Select **Alternating Stress Mean Stress**. S-N Data appear on the right side of the screen.

The figure below displays the **S-N curve** data. Note that the last entry is **86.2 MPa** at **10^6 cycles**.

	B	C
1	Cycles	Alternating Stress (Pa)
2	10	3.999E+09
3	20	2.827E+09
4	50	1.896E+09
5	100	1.413E+09
6	200	1.069E+09
7	2000	4.41E+08
8	10000	2.62E+08
9	20000	2.14E+08
10	1E+05	1.38E+08
11	2E+05	1.14E+08
12	1E+06	8.62E+07
*		

Figure 6-32 Alternating stress curve data.

Insert Life and Safety Factor in the Fatigue Tool

8. Fatigue Tool > Contour Results > Life

9. Fatigue Tool > Contour Results > Safety Factor

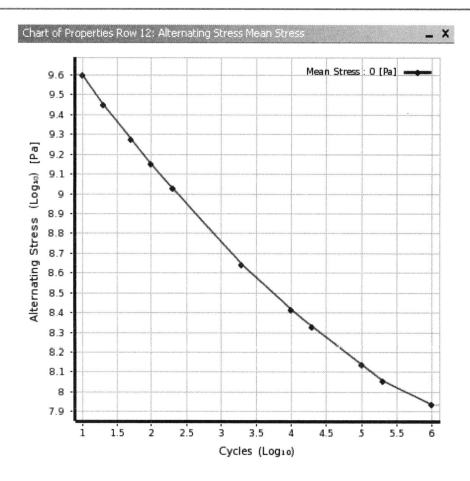

Figure 6-33 Structural steel alternating stress curve.

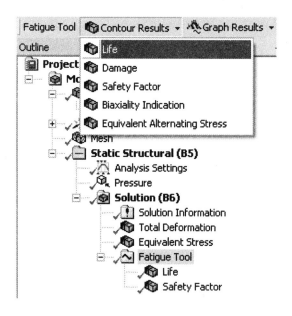

Figure 6-34 Insert Life object in Fatigue Tool.

Initiating **solve** will compute the stress state in the part and evaluate the fatigue state using the material properties given.

10.   Solve   ⌇ Solve

Note that the computed result for the **Equivalent Stress is exactly the same** as in Tutorial 6A. Nothing has changed in the loading and geometry.

However, we want to evaluate the fatigue response to a **completely reversed loading** as interpreted by the **Fatigue Tool**. See the figure below.

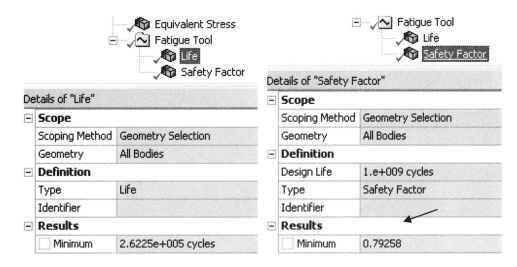

Figure 6-35 Completely reversed loading fatigue tool results.

The maximum von Mises stress for the part is **109 MPa**. The lowest point on the S-N data is **86.2 MPa**. So the part will not have infinite life.

These results indicate that for the stress level and completely reversed nature of the loading the estimated **part life** is about **2.6e5 cycles**. This represents a **safety factor** of **0.79** (86.2/109) with respect to a target life of 1.e9 cycles. That is, this design won't make the target life unless it's bigger, the stress concentration is reduced, the load is reduced, its characteristics are changed, the material is changed, or some combination of these.

The applied load is **100 kN** in magnitude. In the simulation above the loading is **completely reversed**. That is, it varies from +100 kN to 0 to -100 kN to 0, etc as shown in the Fatigue Tool Loading Options figure above.

Repeated Loading

Suppose instead of the above scenario that the load is repeated; that is, it varies from +100 kN to 0 to +100 kN and never goes negative. We can consider that case by changing the **Type** to **Zero-Based** and the **Mean Stress Theory** to **Goodman** in the Details of "**Fatigue Tool**" as depicted below.

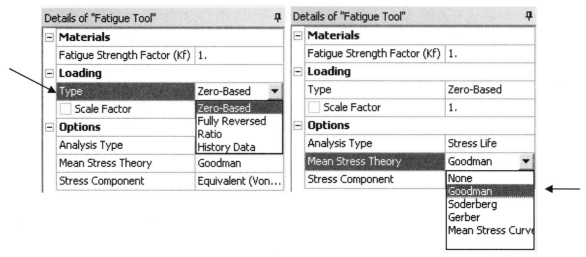

Figure 6-36 Repeated loading.

The Goodman method relates the mean value of the stress to the ultimate strength of the material and the oscillatory component to the fatigue strength of the material. See a good discussion on fatigue design.

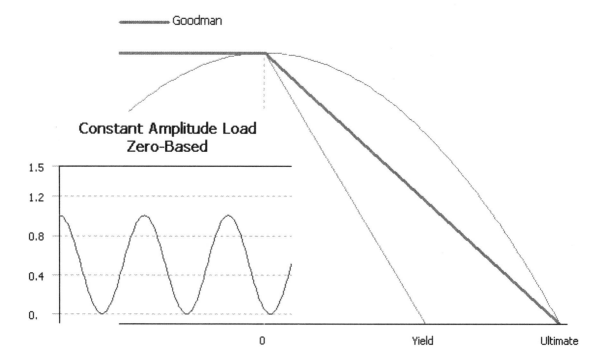

Figure 6-37 Repeated loading with Goodman line.

We now want to **re-evaluate the results**.

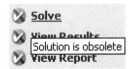

The simulation wizard warns that the current solution is obsolete.

11.   Solve   Solve

The fatigue tool results are shown in the figure that follows.

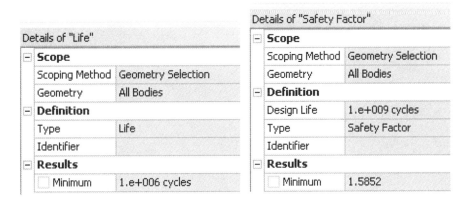

Figure 6-38 Repeated loading fatigue tool results.

The repeated loading is not as severe as the completely reversed loading on the same part. The mean stress and the stress amplitude are both 109/2 = **54.5 MPa** for this condition.

The life is 10^6 cycles, essentially infinite, and the safety factor, *SF*, is 1.58 as computed using the material ultimate tensile strength (**450 MPa**) combined with the material fatigue strength at 10^6 cycles (**86.2 MPa**).

$$\frac{1}{SF} = \frac{\sigma_m}{S_u} + \frac{\sigma_a}{S_e} = \frac{54.5}{450} + \frac{54.5}{86.2}$$

The fatigue tool provides a number of other types of fatigue process modeling. Again, see a good reference on this complex subject for a complete interpretation of computed results.

6-6 SUMMARY

Chapter 6 tutorials introduce the use of ANSYS Mechanical Wizards and Tools and illustrate their use with problems involving static loads with parts made of ductile materials and parts made of brittle materials. A different failure criterion is used in each case. Also considered are problems of a fatigue nature where the load is fluctuating with time the fatigue characteristics of the material become important considerations.

6-7 PROBLEMS

In the problems below use ANSYS to compute the required maximum stress value(s). Use these FEM computed values to determine by hand calculation the requested factors and margins of safety. Then use ANSYS Tools to compute these factors and margins of safety and compare your results.

6-1 Find the **minimum factor of safety** against yielding for the modified plate with the square hole of Tutorial 4B (include the 15 mm radius) if it is made of the default structural steel and carries a static axial load of 100 kN, (50 kN on the quadrant shown).

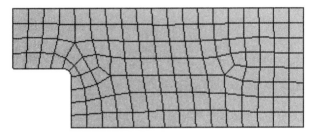

Figure P6-1

6-2 Repeat Problem 6-1 but let the material be the gray cast iron used in Tutorial 6B of this chapter and the **failure by brittle fracture**.

6-3 Consider the Problem 6-1 with the part made of steel and find its **life** if the applied load is completely reversed.

6-4 Consider the Problem 6-1 with the part made of steel and find its life if the applied **load is repeated**, i.e., varies from zero to its maximum positive value back to zero then to its maximum positive value again without becoming negative.

6-5 Find the minimum factor of safety against yielding for the pressure vessel of Tutorial 5A under static loading conditions if it is made of the default structural steel.

6-6 Find the minimum **factor of safety** for the pressure vessel of Tutorial 5A under static loading conditions if it is made of the gray cast iron used in Tutorial 6B of this chapter.

Figure P6-6

NOTES:

Chapter 7

Heat Transfer &

Thermal Stress

7-1 OVERVIEW

In previous chapters we have considered problems in structural and continuum mechanics; however ANSYS Workbench capabilities also include modeling of problems involving the behavior of thermal systems and electromagnetic systems. In this chapter we demonstrate

   ◆ Determining temperature distributions for conduction/convection problems

   ◆ Using temperature distributions to find thermal stresses

7-2 INTRODUCTON

Linear thermal conduction/convection problems are formulated using the finite element approach with temperature as the single degree-of-freedom variable at each node in the mesh and with the material conduction properties used to form the thermal 'stiffness matrix'.

ANSYS Workbench includes capability for modeling many types of thermal and thermal stress problems of interest to practicing engineers. The temperature distributions found at each thermal analysis node can be used with the equivalent structural model as inputs for finding stresses caused by temperature changes.

7-3 HEAT TRANSFER

We start by solving a simple heat transfer problem involving conduction as well as convection and select a problem for which we have a theoretical solution readily available for comparison.

7-4   TUTORIAL 7A – TEMPERATURE DISTRIBUTION IN A CYLINDER

Objective: We wish to compute the temperature distribution in a long steel cylinder with inner radius 5 inches and outer radius 10 inches. The **interior surface** of the cylinder is kept at **75 deg F**, and heat is lost on the **exterior** by **convection** to a fluid whose temperature is **40 deg F**. The **convection coefficient is 2.0e-4 BTU/sec-sq.in-F** and the **thermal conductivity** for steel is taken to be **8.09e-4 BTU/sec-in-F** (the default value for structural steel).

1.   **We first create the geometry associated with this tutorial problem.** For analysis of the long cylinder, the length of the model we create is arbitrary since every section along the length behaves like every other section. For this tutorial we'll use a segment that is **1.0 inch long**.

Figure 7-1 Segment of cylinder one inch in length.

2.   Start **ANSYS Workbench** > use **DesignModeler** to **create the geometry** or to **attach a previously created solid model. Save** the **Workbench** file as **T7A.**

3.   **Add Steady-State Thermal Analysis to the Project Schematic. Share the geometry.**

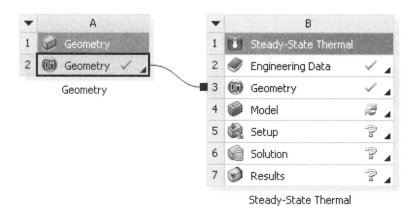

Figure 7-2 Steady-State Thermal Analysis in the Project Schematic.

4. Double click **Model** to start **Mechanical Steady State Thermal Analysis**

5. **Units > U. S. Customary (in, lbm, lbf, °F, s, V, A)** Verify the units.

6. **Verify material** properties for **Structural Steel**

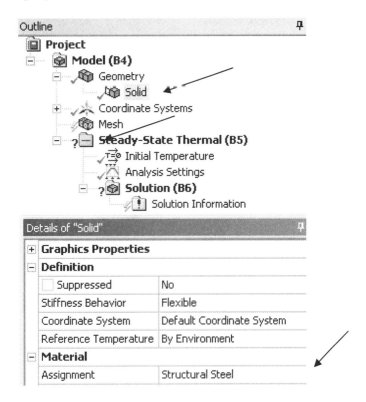

Figure 7-3 Material properties.

Apply the **temperature boundary condition** to the interior surface.

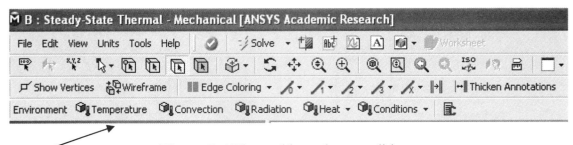

Figure 7-4 Thermal boundary conditions.

7. **Environment > Temperature; Select inner surface > Apply > Magnitude 75 F**

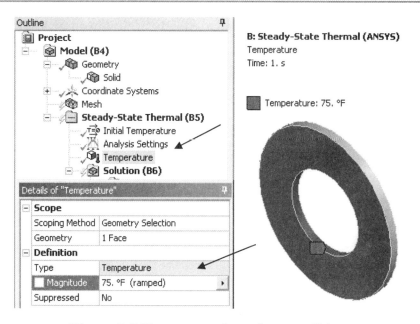

Figure 7-5 Temperature boundary condition.

Apply the **convection condition** on the exterior surface.

8.　　**Environment > Thermal > Convection;** Select the outer surface **Geometry Selection > Apply**

9.　　**Details of "Convection" > Film Coefficient > 2.e-4 BTU/s in² F**

10.　**Details of "Convection" > Ambient Temperature > 40 F**

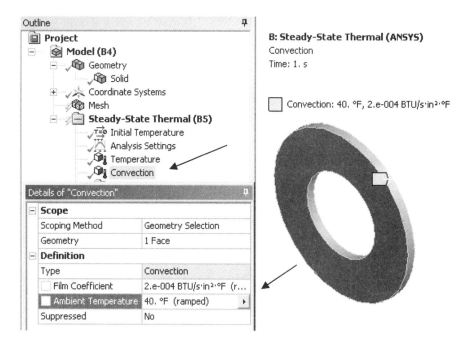

Figure 7-6 Convection boundary conditions.

Since each cross section along the length of the cylinder behaves in the same way, the front and back surfaces of the washer model are given **perfect insulation** boundary conditions to prevent any heat transfer in our model in the direction along the length of the cylinder.

11.   **Environment > Heat > Perfectly Insulated** (Select the **front face**; Ctrl Select the **back face**.)

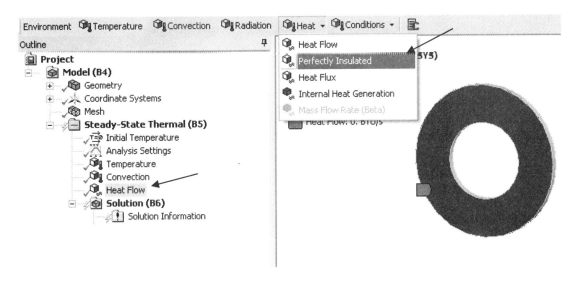

Figure 7-7 Perfect insulation condition.

Add Temperature as the solution quantity to be determined.

12.   **Solution > Thermal > Temperature**

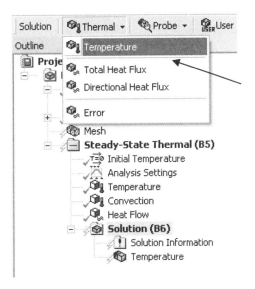

Figure 7-8 Temperature solution quantity.

13.   **Solution > Solve** (Solve the problem)   Solve

The computed temperature distribution is shown in the next figure.

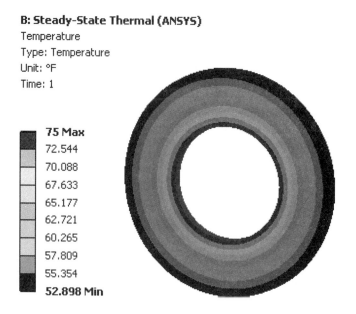

Figure 7-9 Temperature distribution.

The maximum temperature is on the interior and is the specified **75 F** as expected, and on the outside wall the minimum temperature is found to be almost **53 F**. Insert **the thermal error object.**

14.   Solution > Thermal > Error

The default mesh for this problem together with the thermal error distribution is displayed in the figure that follows. The estimated energy of the error in the solution ranges from around 3e-9 to 1.2e-6 BTU. These small error estimates give us confidence in the results of this simulation. Select **Solution Information**, page down **Solid90**.

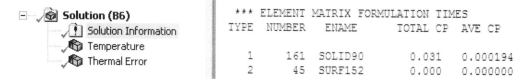

Figure 7-10 Solid90 information.

Steady State Thermal > Help > Mechanical Help > Search > Solid90. Tell us that Solid90 is a **20-node thermal element** with midside nodes and curved edges.

The results for this sample problem can be verified using closed form solutions from heat transfer theory, and we find that the computed surface temperature is very accurate.

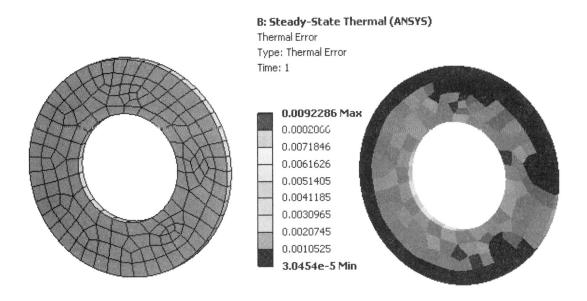

Figure 7-11 Problem mesh and thermal error distribution.

Because of its symmetry, this problem could have been solved with a much smaller model, say a small wedge with the cut faces perfectly insulated. Try it.

Figure 7-12 Wedge model.

7-5   THERMAL STRESS I

The **objective** of the second tutorial of this chapter is to **determine the stresses** in an object caused by a **uniform temperature change**.

When a temperature change occurs in an object, its coefficient of thermal expansion causes an expansion or contraction of the object depending upon whether the temperature increases or decreases. If the object is uniform and unrestrained, there is no stress associated with this free motion. On the other hand, if the object is subject to restraint against the thermally induced movement, a stress will occur.

ANSYS Workbench provides tools for the solution of thermal stress problems of various types. The temperature changes can be uniform throughout the body or distributed due to thermal conditions such as the temperature distribution in the previous tutorial. First we consider a uniform temperature change.

7-6   TUTORIAL 7B – UNIFORM TEMPERATURE CHANGE

Consider a block of material surrounded by a second material as shown in the figure below. The composite object is subjected to a temperature change so that both regions attain a uniform final temperature throughout. **Find the deformations and stresses** that result if the initial state is stress free. We're missing a couple of components here, but this is similar to the situation that occurs when **silicon** computer chips (1) are encapsulated with **epoxy** polymer (2).

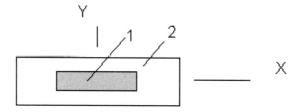

Figure 7-13 Encapsulation model.

Figure 7-14 15 x 10 x 2 mm silicon chip and 25 x 15 x 6 mm epoxy encapsulation.

For our model we assume a representative geometry of about **15 x 10 x 2 mm** for the silicon item being encapsulated. After encapsulation the **package size** is **25 x 15 x 6 mm**.

The properties for the materials are given in the table below. Here **CTE** is the **Coefficient of Thermal Expansion**.

Material Properties

	Elastic Modulus	Poisson's Ratio	CTE
Silicon	190 GPa	0.28	2.34 E –6 /C
Epoxy	13 GPa	0.30	1.69 E –5/C

We consider the case in which the epoxy and silicon experience a temperature change of **-150 deg C** during cool down of the molding process.

The package was modeled as an **assembly** in **Pro/ENGINEER** and is shown below.

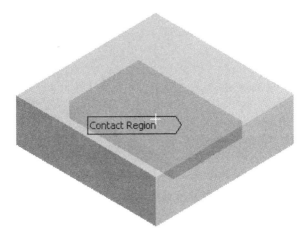

Figure 7-15 The assembled chip/epoxy package.

Before importing into ANSYS Workbench however, we will isolate an **octant of the package** and make use of **symmetry** in the geometry and loading. The next figure shows the Pro/E model of an octant of the package after the rest of the solid has been trimmed away.

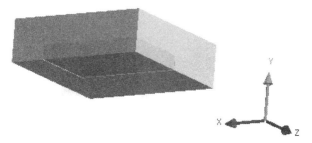

Figure 7-16 Octant of the package.

The portion selected for analysis lies in the octant defined by the positive X, Y and Z axes. Symmetric deformation requires that no movement across the planes of symmetry be allowed.

1.   **Start ANSYS Workbench** > use **DesignModeler** to **create** or **attach to the geometry**

This is a **Structural Problem** with a **Thermal Loading**; not a thermal problem. Add **Static Structural** to the Project Schematic and share the geometry.

2.   **Static Structural**

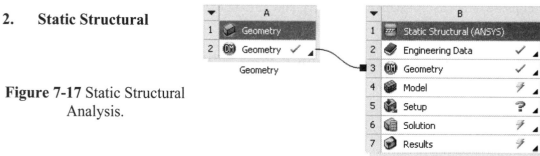

Figure 7-17 Static Structural
          Analysis.

The   interfacial   boundary
between silicon and epoxy is defined automatically in ANSYS Mechanical by a **contact region**. A number of different contact models are provided for use (Chapter 5), and in our case we accept the default of **bonded contact**. This means that the surfaces are bonded together and do not separate or slide upon one another. This behavior best describes the case for the encapsulation model we are building. The component parts of our Pro/E model were named **OUTSIDEPART** and **CHIP**.

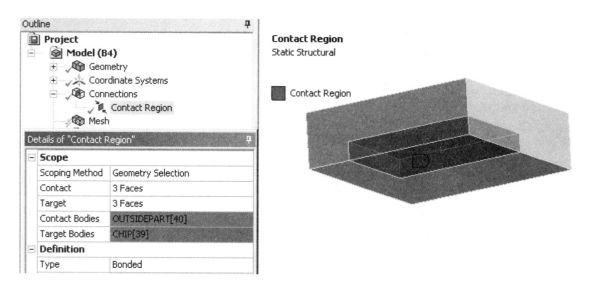

Figure 7-18 Contact surfaces of model.

Next we need to define the structural properties for **silicon** and **epoxy materials**.

3.   **Double Click Engineering Data** in the **Project Schematic**, cell **B2**

Be sure **View > Properties & Outline** are selected.

Turn **Engineering Data Sources off**. 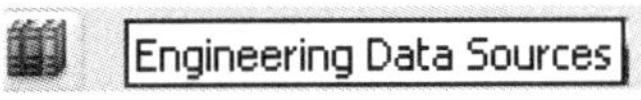 [Engineering Data Sources]

Select Engineering Data and Select **Click here to add a new material.**

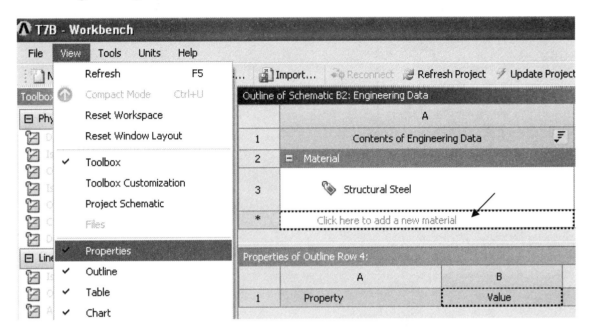

Figure 7-19 Engineering material data.

4.   **Type Silicon** for the **new material name**.

5.   **Expand** the **Toolbox** items **Physical Properties** and **Linear Elastic**.

6.   Double click **Isotropic Instantaneous Coefficient of Thermal Expansion** to add it to the **CTE Properties of Silicon, 2.34e-6 & 22**

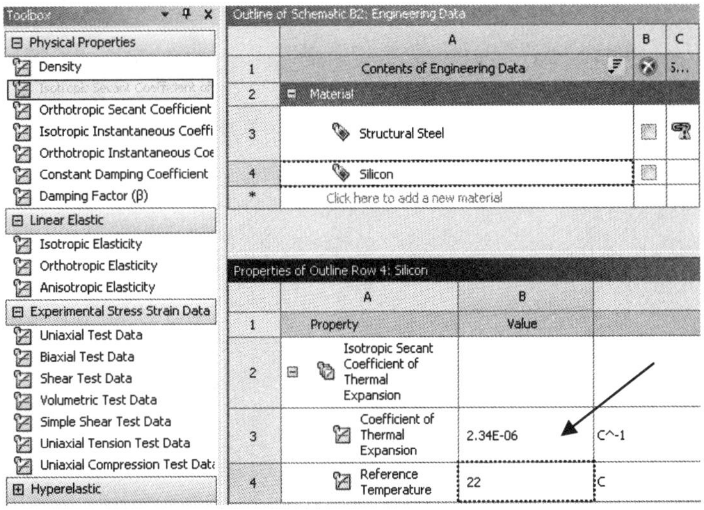

Figure 7-20 Silicon CTE data.

7.   Do the same for **Isotropic Elasticity**

Enter 1.9e11 and 0.28

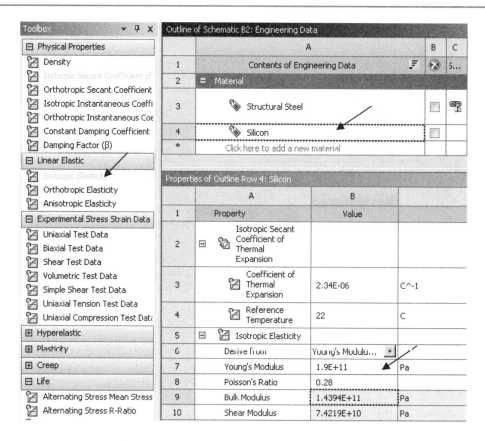

Figure 7-21 Define properties for Silicon

8. **Do the same for the Epoxy properties. Return to Project**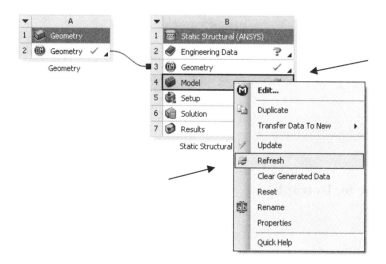

9. **Right** click on **Model** and **Select Refresh** to **add the new materials to the project.**

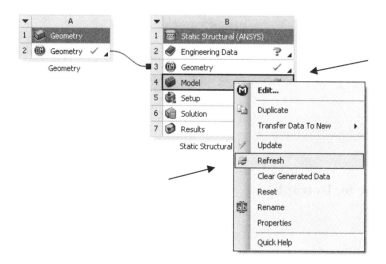

Figure 7-22 Refresh the project.

10. **Return** to **Mechanical** and **assign Epoxy** to the **OUTSIDEPART**

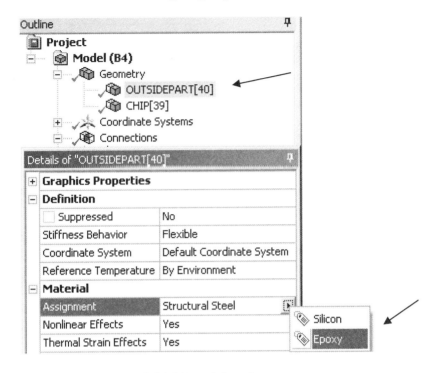

Figure 7-23 Material assignment.

11. **Assign Silicon** to the **CHIP**

In this tutorial we have a structural model subjected to a thermal environment. The package is stress free when the temperature is 150 deg C. It then cools down to room temperature 22 deg C. The **whole package** gets the same temperature change. Change the stress free reference temperature to 150 deg C.

12. **Details of Static Structural > Environmental Temperature > 150 C**

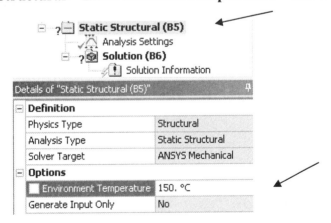

Figure 7-24 Stress free reference temperature.

Apply the final **uniform** room temperature as a thermal condition.

13.   Environment > Loads >Thermal Condition = 22 C.
Be sure the volume selection filter is on
and Ctrl select both solids in the model > **Apply**.

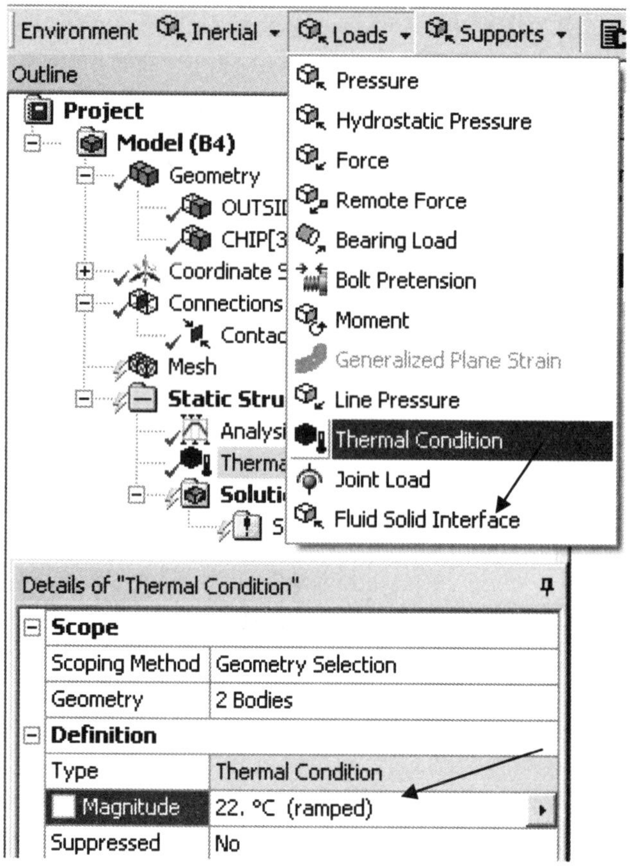

Figure 7-25 Thermal condition.

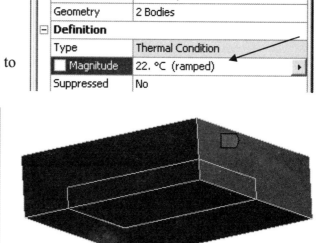

Now apply **Frictionless Support** displacement boundary conditions to prevent movement of the model in a direction perpendicular to the planes of symmetry.

14.   Environment > Supports > Frictionless Supports (Use Ctrl to chain select six faces.)

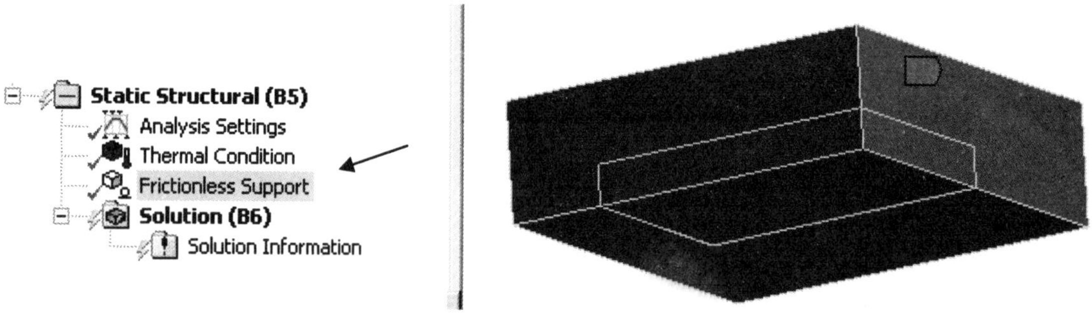

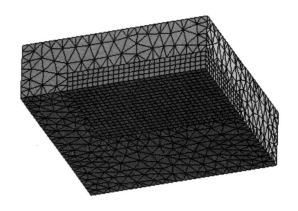

Figure 7-26 Displacement boundary condition.

Create the Size > Medium default mesh.

Figure 7-27 Default mesh.

Add the **maximum principal stress**, the **total deformation**, and the **stress error** to the solution items.

15.   **Solution > Stress > Maximum Principal**

16.   **Solution > Deformation > Total**

17.   **Solution > Stress > Error**

18.   **Solve**   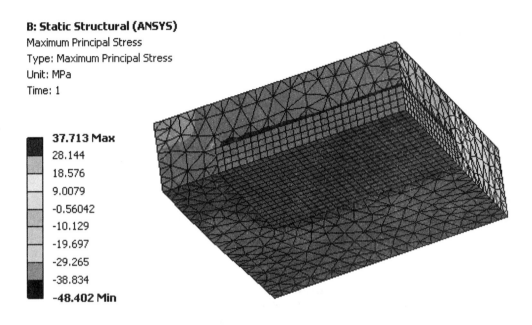 Solve

View the maximum principal stress distribution from the bottom side of the octant.

Figure 7-28 Maximum principal stress.

The coefficient of thermal expansion of the epoxy is seven times greater than that of silicon, so the epoxy shrinks at a greater rate than the silicon during the process of cooling. That puts the silicon in compression and the epoxy in tension and is reflected in the stress distributions shown above.

To better see what's going on we will **hide the chip** component and view the stresses in the epoxy.

19.   Right click **Chip > Hide Body**.

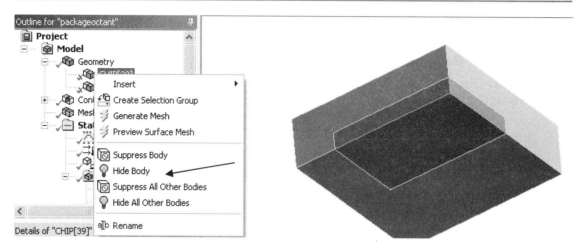

Figure 7-29 Hide the chip component.

Then display the **maximum principal stress**.

20.   Solution > Maximum Principal Stress

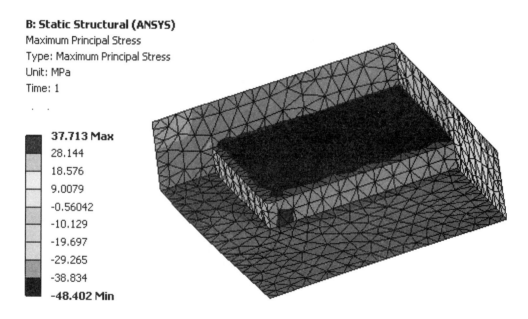

Figure 7-30 Maximum principal stress in epoxy component.

Next display the **structural error**.

21.   Solution > Structural Error

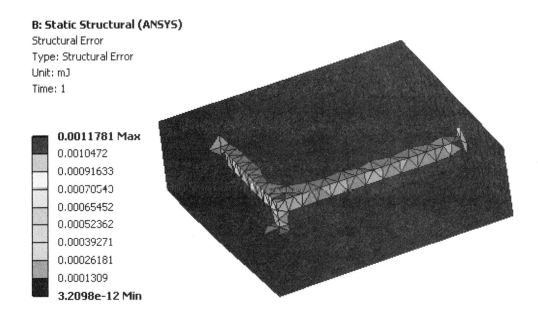

B: Static Structural (ANSYS)
Structural Error
Type: Structural Error
Unit: mJ
Time: 1

0.0011781 Max
0.0010472
0.00091633
0.00070540
0.00065452
0.00052362
0.00039271
0.00026181
0.0001309
3.2098e-12 Min

Figure 7-31 Structural error in the epoxy component.

Note that the errors are large along the interior edge and highest at the corner where the two edges meet. These are regions of singularity because of the zero radius geometry. If we want good stress estimates for this component, we will need to include the actual corner radius at these locations.

Unhide the chip and **hide the epoxy portion**.

22. Right click **CHIP > Show Body**.

Insert ▶
Create Selection Group
Solve

Suppress Body
Suppress All Other Bodies
Show Body

Show All Bodies

Rename

Figure 7-32 Show body option.

23. Right click **OUTSIDEPART > Hide Body**.

B: Static Structural (ANSYS)
Maximum Principal Stress
Type: Maximum Principal Stress
Unit: MPa
Time: 1

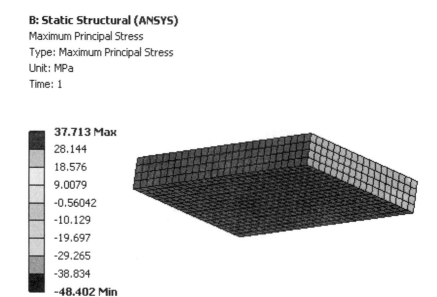

37.713 Max	
28.144	
18.576	
9.0079	
-0.56042	
-10.129	
-19.697	
-29.265	
-38.834	
-48.402 Min	

Figure 7-33 Maximum principal stress in the chip.

24. Right click in the model display area > **Isometric View**

This shows the chip from the top, and the corner region of maximum compressive stress is evident.

25. Display Total Deformation (Show Undeformed Wireframe) **Save your work.**

B: Static Structural (ANSYS)
Total Deformation
Type: Total Deformation
Unit: mm
Time: 1

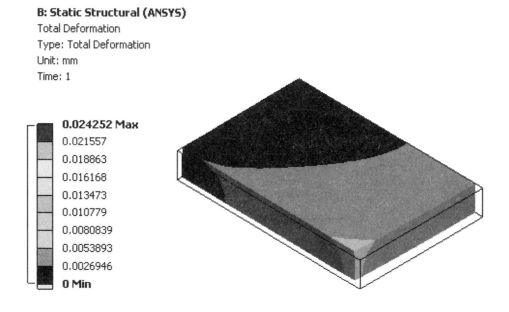

0.024252 Max	
0.021557	
0.018863	
0.016168	
0.013473	
0.010779	
0.0080839	
0.0053893	
0.0026946	
0 Min	

Figure 7-34 Total deformation in the chip.

Stresses and deformations computed for the chip with this mesh should be reasonably accurate as are the deformations computed for the epoxy portion and stresses in the epoxy portion at locations removed from the singularities.

7-7 THERMAL STRESS II

In tutorial **T7C** we will determine the stresses that are produced in a cylinder by an **internal pressure** acting together with a **temperature variation** through the wall thickness similar to the one we calculated in tutorial T7A.

Consider the same 5 inch interior radius, 10 inch exterior radius **steel cylinder** as considered in tutorial T7A. The cylinder is subjected to an internal **pressure of 300 psi**. The **internal surface temperature is 480 deg F** and the **external surface temperature is 77 deg F**. The **objective** is to find stress distribution and the magnitude and location of the **maximum von Mises stress**.

7-8 TUTORIAL 7C – THERMAL STRESS IN A CYLINDER

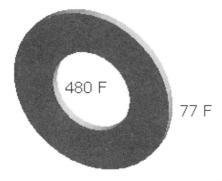

Figure 7-35 Temperature boundary conditions.

1.   **Start ANSYS Workbench** > use **DesignModeler** to **create** or to **attach geometry.**

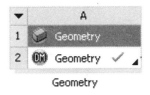

Figure 7-36 DesignModeler in Project Schematic.

2.   **Toolbox > Custom Systems > Thermal-Stress**. Add the Thermal-Stress Analysis

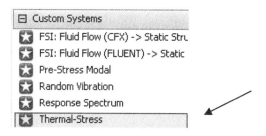

Figure 7-37 Thermal-Stress Analysis.

The Custom System Thermal-Stress inserts both the Steady-State Thermal and the Static Structural Analysis systems into the Project tree.

3.   Share the Geometry

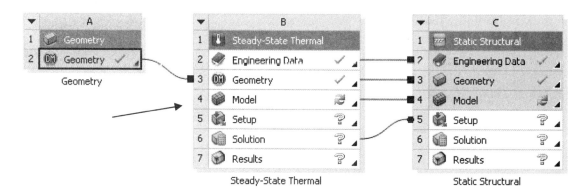

Figure 7-38 Thermal-Stress Modules in the Project Schematic.

4.   Double click Steady-State Thermal Model cell (B4)

The Outline Tree contains **both Steady-State Thermal** and **Static Structural Analysis** objects. We apply **thermal** and **structural boundary conditions** and **loads**

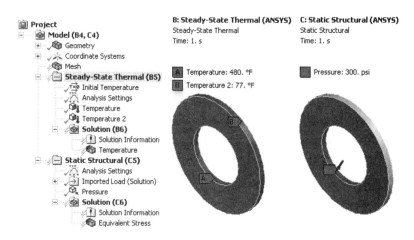

Figure 7-39 Outline, Thermal and Structural conditions.

THERMAL CONDITIONS

5.   Steady-State Thermal > Initial Condition > 71.6 deg F (default ambient).

6.   Environment > Temperature Select the inside surface of the cylinder.

7.   Details of "Temperature" > Geometry > Apply

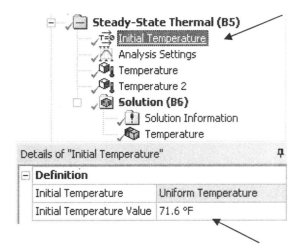

Figure 7-40 Initial Temperature.

8.   Details of "Temperature" > Magnitude > 480 F

9.   Apply the 77 F condition to the exterior surface.

Find the temperature distribution in the disk.

10.   Steady-State Thermal > Solution > Solve

The next figure shows the temperature distribution, and note that the correct boundary temperatures of 480 F and 75 F are displayed as expected.

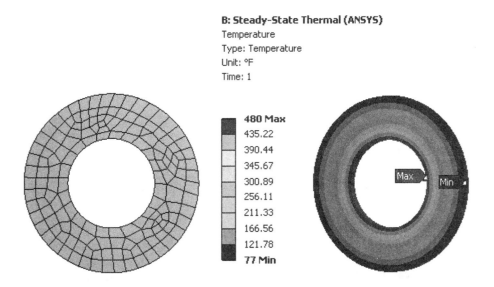

Figure 7-41 Default mesh and temperature distribution from Thermal Solution.

Use the probe option ⌨Probe to determine the temperature near the point midway through the wall of the cylinder. The computed temperature here agrees well with the analytical solution to this problem.

STRUCTURAL CONDITIONS

Accept the default reference temperature of 71.6 deg F and apply the structural loads.

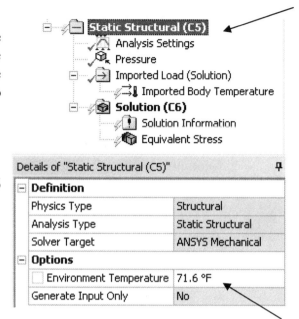

Figure 7-42 Initial Temperature.

11.   **Environment > Structural > Pressure** Select the inside surface of the cylinder.

12.   **Details of "Pressure" > Geometry > Apply**

13.   **Details of "Pressure" > Magnitude > 300 psi**

Right click on **Steady-State Thermal** object **(B5)** and rename as **Disk Thermal Problem** in the **Outline.**

The figure below shows that the **Temperature Distribution** from the **Disk Thermal Problem Solution** will be **imported** for use in the **solution** of the **Static Structural Problem.** Note dashed line.

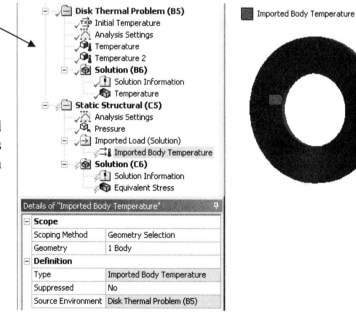

Figure 7-43 Disk Thermal Prob.

If you have not done already, add the **von Mises** Equivalent Stress quantity to the computed solution quantities.

14.   **Solution > Stress > Equivalent (von-Mises)**

15.   Right click **Static Structural Solution > Solve** ⌁Solve

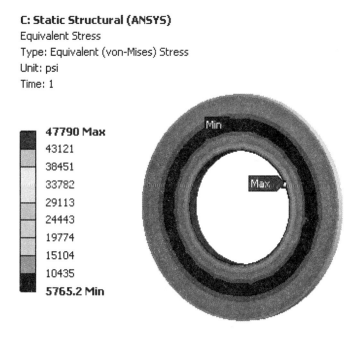

C: Static Structural (ANSYS)
Equivalent Stress
Type: Equivalent (von-Mises) Stress
Unit: psi
Time: 1

47790 Max
43121
38451
33782
29113
24443
19774
15104
10435
5765.2 Min

Figure 7-44 Computed von Mises Stress.

The response of a structural system to **static** loads requires that displacement boundary constraints be applied to restrain the motion of the object as a rigid body, otherwise the applied loads cause motion to occur and the problem becomes a problem in **dynamics**. Normally these restraints are obvious from the problem setting (a building is fixed to the ground, a part is restrained by the parts to which it is joined, etc.).

We applied no constraints in the current tutorial; the simulation software recognized the possibility of rigid body motion and applied some **weak springs** to restrain the rigid body motion. The warning shown below is issued so the user can make adjustments to the model if necessary. In our case the weak springs work just fine, so we continue with the evaluation of the computed results.

Messages	
	Text
Warning	One or more bodies may be underconstrained and experiencing rigid body motion. Weak springs have been added

Figure 7-45 Weak spring warning.

The figure above shows that the maximum von Mises stress occurs at the interior surface of the cylinder and has a value of **47,790 psi**. The value on the outer surface is about **30,900 psi**.

16.   Save your work.

The stress contours are a little ragged indicating that a refined mesh should be used to give more accurate answers.

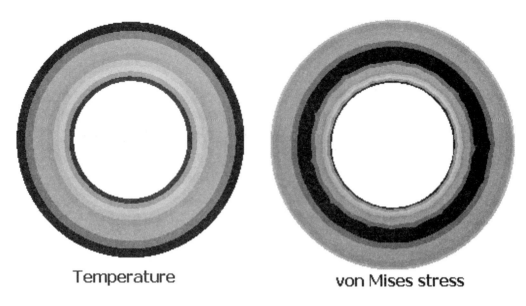

Temperature   von Mises stress

Figure 7-46 Temperature and von Mises stress distributions using the default mesh.

It is interesting to note the computed temperature distribution contours (Figure above left) are quite smooth while the stress contours are not. This is because in general a finer mesh is required for an accurate solution to the stress problem than is required for an accurate solution to the temperature problem, something to keep in mind when constructing the initial mesh for problems of this type. We could go back and refine the mesh and re-evaluate the results, but we'll leave that for one of the problems at the end of the chapter.

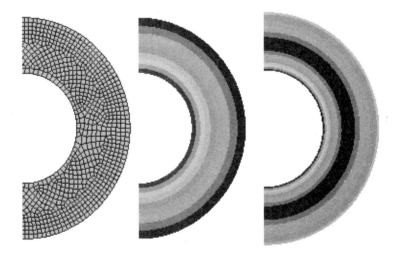

Figure 7-47 Temperature and von Mises stress distributions for a finer mesh.

Also note that the Custom Thermal-Stress Analysis module is configured to automatically solve the Thermal Problem first and then transfer the temperature distribution to the Static Structural Problem. It's not necessary to manually solve the

Thermal Problem first; you can set up all components of the Thermal-Stress problem, than select Solve from the top menu.

7-9 SUMMARY

The tutorials in this chapter illustrate the solution of thermal conduction/convection problems as well as the determination of thermal stresses arising from uniform or non-uniform temperature distributions. Problems such as these arise very often in engineering practice.

7-10 PROBLEMS

7-1 An 8 in diameter steel disk 0.25 inches in thickness has a 2 in diameter hole located 2 inches radially from its center. The surface of the hole is maintained at 75 F, and the exterior surface is kept at 32 F. The front and back surfaces are perfectly insulated.

Find the magnitude and location of the maximum **von Mises stress**, the maximum **principal stress**, and the maximum **principal strain** if the disk is initially in a stress-free state at 73 F before the thermal conditions are applied.

Figure P7-1

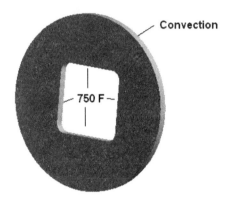
Figure P7-3

7-2 Solve problem 7-1 using the exterior convection conditions of Tutorial T7A.

7-3 A 20 inch diameter cylinder has an 8 in square hole with 1.0 inch radius corner fillets. Model as a 2D problem assuming perfect insulation on the front and back faces of the 1.0 inch slice shown. Determine the **temperature distribution** and **maximum principal stress** magnitude if the interior surface of the cylinder is kept at 750 deg F and heat is lost on the exterior by convection to a fluid whose temperature is 40 deg F. The convection coefficient is 2.0e-4 BTU/sec-sq.in-F.

7-4 Refine the mesh for Tutorial T7C so as to compute smooth **von Mises stress** contours. **Compare** the maximum and minimum von Mises stress values you compute with those found in the tutorial.

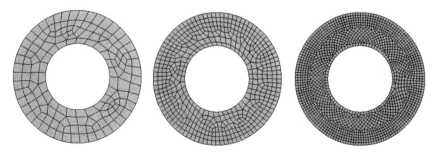
Figure P7-3

7-5 Refine the mesh for Tutorial T7C so as to compute smooth **von Mises stress** contours. Compare the maximum and minimum von Mises stress values you compute with those found in the tutorial.

7-6 A long 6 inch square tube has a 3 inch diameter hole. If 100 degree F gases flow through the inside, and the outside is cooled by convection in air at 0 deg F, plot the resulting temperature distribution and estimate the temperature at the mid point of the thinnest part of the cross section.

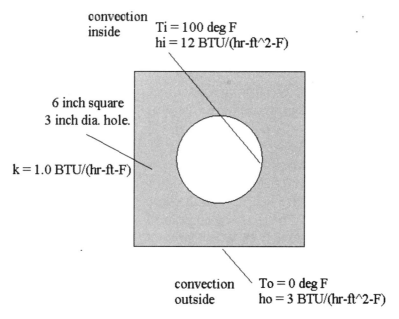

Figure P7-6

7-7 An assembly of two identical bars 2.5 mm in width is shown below. One is made of steel, the other is made of copper alloy; they are bonded together to form a bimetallic strip. The left end is completely fixed. The bar is initially at room temperature then experiences a uniform 25 deg C decrease in temperature.

(a) Find the **maximum vertical displacement** of the tip.

(b) Find the magnitude and location of the **maximum von Mises stress** in the **fillet** area.

(c) Find the magnitude and location of the **maximum principal strain** in the **fillet** area.

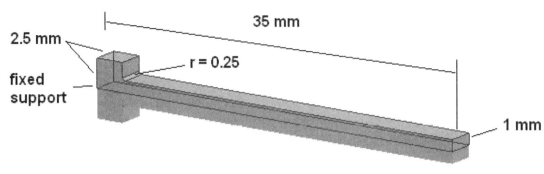

Figure P7-7

7-8 Find the magnitude of the **temperature in the middle of the thinnest portion of the cross section** of the circular ring shown. The ring has an internal circular cavity. The ring and its cross section are shown below. Material properties are: E = 2e11 Pa, nu = 0.3, CTE = 12e-6 m/m-C, KXX = 50 W/m-C.

Gases on the **interior hole** maintain the hole surface temperature at **100 deg C**. The **outside** surface of the ring transfers heat by **convection** to the surrounding fluid whose temperature is **35 deg C**. The **film coefficient is 15 W/m^2-C.**

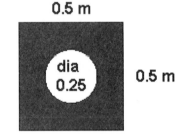

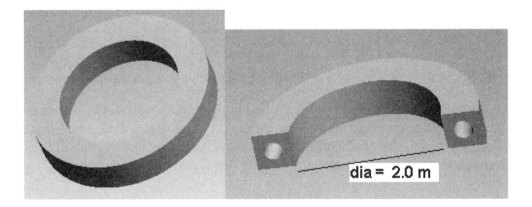

Figure P7-8

7-9 The structural steel bar is 8 x 1.5 x 0.4 inches. The central hole is 0.6 x 0.6 with 0.1 inch fillet radii. One end is kept at 300 deg F while all other surfaces convect heat to the surrounding 0 deg F air. The film coefficient is 2e-5 BTU/s in^2 F. The bar is initially at room temperature 72F.

(a) Determine the **difference in temperature** between the **left** and **right inside surfaces** of the **rectangular cutout**.

(b) Find the **magnitude and location** of the **maximum principal strain** that occurs.

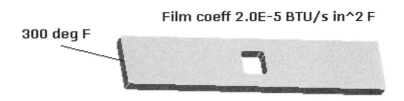

Figure P7-9

7-10 The structural steel bar is 8 x 1.5 x 0.4 inches. The central hole is 0.6 x 0.6 with 0.1 inch fillet radii. One end is kept at 300 deg F while all other surfaces convect heat to the surrounding 0 deg F air. The film coefficient is 2e-5 BTU/s in^2 F. The bar is initially at room temperature 72F.

NOTES:

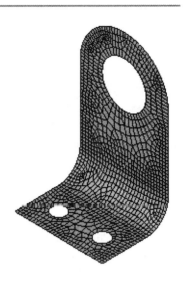

Chapter 8

Surface & Line Models

8-1 OVERVIEW

This chapter discusses structural and thermal simulation response of problems that can be analyzed with surface or line models. These include:

- ♦ Plane stress, plane strain or axisymmetric problems

- ♦ Plate (shell) problems

- ♦ Line-body (beam element) problems

8-2 INTRODUCTION

Surface models are often easier to develop and easier to solve than solid models and can be employed in many practical situations **if** they can accurately represent the behavior of the object under consideration. We are interested in **two-dimensional surface models** for plane stress, plane strain, or axisymmetric analysis and **three-dimensional surface models** for plate analysis.

A state of **plane stress** exists in a thin object loaded in the plane of its largest dimensions. Let the *X-Y* plane be the plane of analysis. The non-zero stresses σ_x, σ_y and τ_{xy} lie in the *X-Y* plane and do not vary in the *Z* direction. Further, the other stresses (σ_z, τ_{yz} and τ_{zx}) are all zero for this kind of geometry and loading. A thin beam loaded in its plane and a thin spur gear tooth are good examples of plane stress problems.

Problems in **plane strain** are typically objects with large dimensions in the *Z* direction relative to its dimensions in the X-Y plane that have loadings uniformly distributed in the *Z* direction and restrained from *Z* motion at its ends. A retaining wall is a common example.

A problem in which the geometry, loadings, boundary conditions and material properties are symmetric with respect to an axis is one that can be solved with an **axisymmetric** finite element model.

Plate or **shell** structural components are surfaces that resist loads applied normal and parallel to their surfaces and provide resistance to bending and in-plane deformation similar to beam components. The plate surface of the deck of a ship is a typical example.

8-3 TUTORIAL 8A – SHEET WITH CIRCLUAR HOLE – PLANE STRESS

In this tutorial we will use ANSYS Mechanical to compute the maximum stress in the thin steel sheet with a central hole considered in **Tutorial T4A**. The object is loaded in the long direction by forces applied at each end. Its dimensions are 1000 mm long, 400 mm high and 10 mm thick. The central circular hole is 200 mm in diameter as shown below.

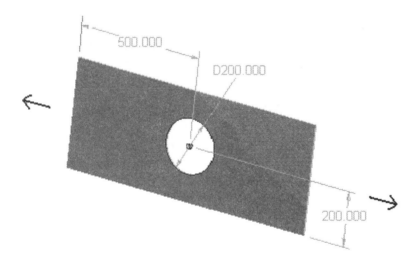

Figure 8-1 Thin sheet with central hole.

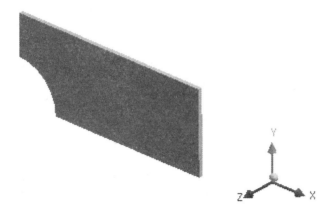

Figure 8-2 Quadrant of sheet.

We need a **surface model** of the **T4A** plate. The solid model for the plate can be created in DesignModeler or in another solid modeler and brought into DesignModeler. We show two options below before starting the stress analysis example.

DESIGN MODELER

1. **Start ANSYS Workbench** and **DesignModeler**

2. **Open** the **existing geometry file** for the **quadrant** of the **sheet** or **create a new model** and **click** on the **sketch** used to **extrude** the **solid model.** The **sketch must be** in the **X-Y plane.**

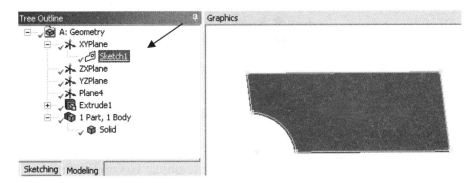

Figure 8-3 Quadrant of sheet in DesignModeler.

3. **Select Sketch1 > Concept > Surfaces From Sketches**

Enter the sheet thickness.

4. **Generate** ⟳ Generate To create the surface.

5. **Details of SurfaceSk1 > 10 mm** (The thickness is carried along with the model but is not used to create geometry. It is just a textual attribute of the planar surface and can be changed at any time.)

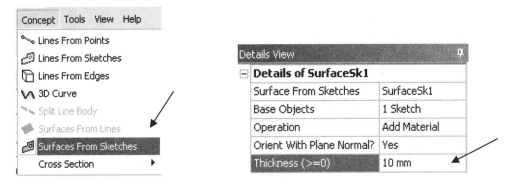

Figure 8-4 Surface creation.

We no longer need the extrusion, so highlight 'Extrude1' and delete it.

6.   Extrude1 > Delete

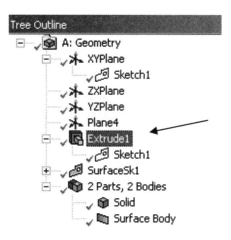

Figure 8-5 Tree outline.

We get the view shown below. The surface geometric object has no thickness.

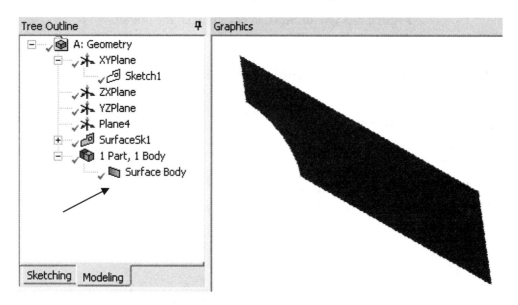

Figure 8-6 Surface model in DesignModeler.

USING ANOTHER SOLID MODELER (Pro/ENGINEER in this case.)

7.   Use an Alternate Solid Modeler to create the **quadrant** of the **plate** with hole.
        Make certain that it is **extruded symmetrically** from a **sketch** in the **XY plane.**

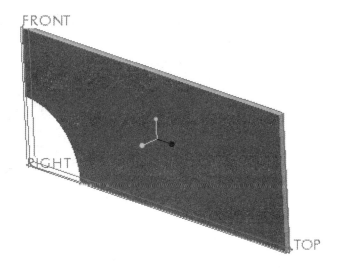

Figure 8-7 Pro/E model extruded symmetrically from a sketch in the XY plane.

8.   Start DesignModeler and attach the **Active CAD Geometry** and **Generate**

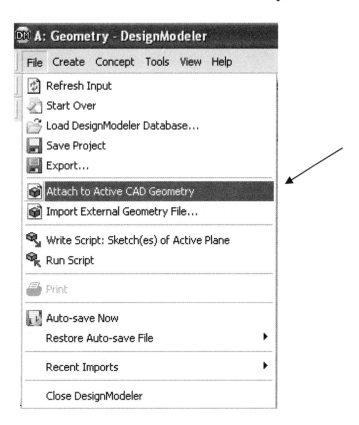

Figure 8-8 Attach geometry in the active solid modeler.

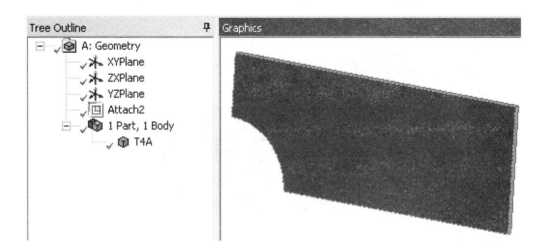

Figure 8-9 Solid model from Pro/E attached in DesignModeler.

Now extract the Middle Surface of this solid.

9.   **DesignModeler > Tools > Mid-Surface**

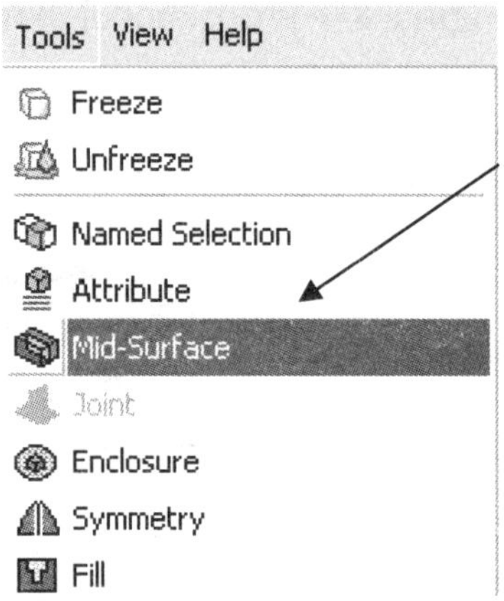

Figure 8-10 Select Tools Mid-Surface.

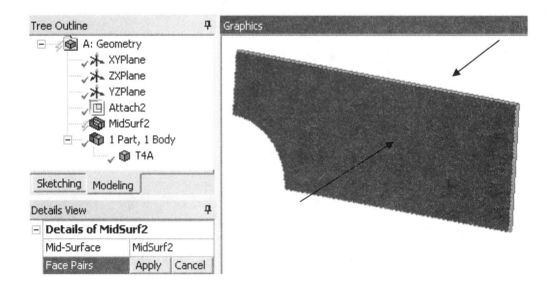

Figure 8-11 Select front and Ctrl select back sides > Apply.

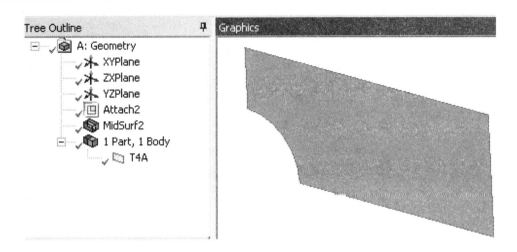

Figure 8-12 Mid-Surface.

BACK TO THE PLANE STRESS EXAMPLE

Now indicate that you're going to use a 2D model for the simulation.

10. On the **Schematic** page, **Select Geometry, cell A2,** then **View > Properties**

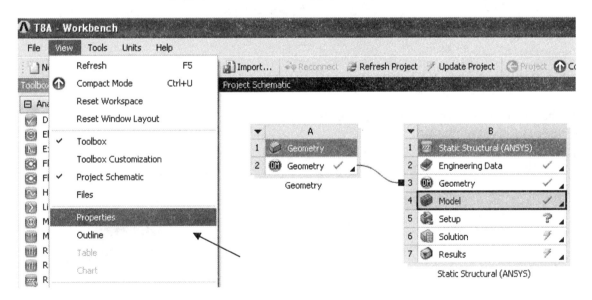

Figure 8-13 View Geometry Properties.

In the Project screen select Advanced Geometry Options; change from 3D to 2D analysis.

11. Advanced Geometry Options > Analysis Type > 2-D (See the next figure.)

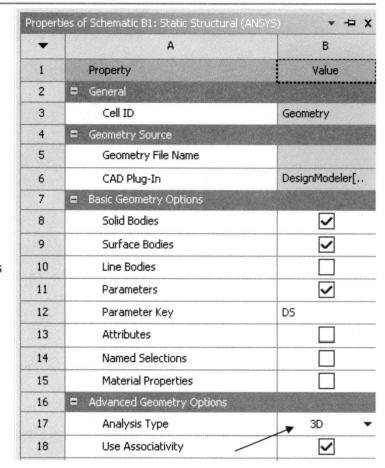

Figure 8-14 Change Analysis Type from 3D to 2D.

12.   **Refresh** the **Model cell B4. Double click Model** to start **Mechanical**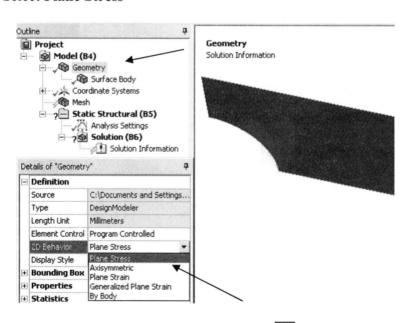

In the details of Geometry Select **Plane Stress**

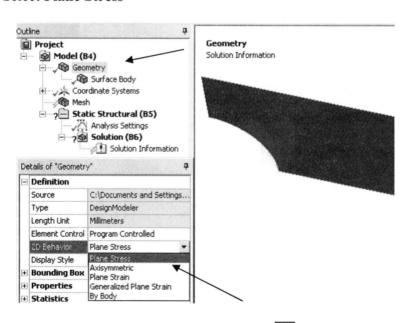

Figure 8-15 2D Behavior - Plane Stress in Mechanical .

Verify that the **units** are **mm, kg, s** and that the material is **structural steel**. Apply **Loads** and **Boundary Conditions**.

Note that the geometry in the simulation is a **surface** (has no geometric thickness), but the **10 mm thickness** for the part is carried forward to the simulation and shows up in the **Details of "Surface Body"** box. The stresses we compute will be inversely proportional to the thickness of the part.

The structural simulation proceeds much as before. We need to first create the **Mesh**, then define the **Environment**, specify the desired **Solution** items to be computed, and then **Solve**. The default material properties for structural steel will be used. We outline the steps in what follows.

13.   **Mesh > Generate Mesh**

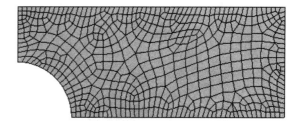

        Figure 8-16 Default 2D mesh.

Loads and boundary conditions are applied to the **edges** of the 2D model.

14.   **Environment > Supports > Frictionless Support**

15.   Click on the **Edge Selection Filter** 🔲.

16.   Select the **Left Edge, Ctrl click Bottom Edge > Apply**

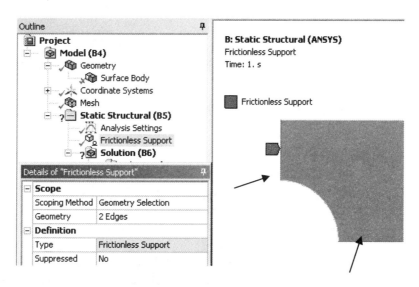

        Figure 8-17 Applying boundary conditions.

Now apply the loading.

17.   **Environment > Loads > Force**

18.   Select the **Right Edge > Apply**

19.   **Magnitude > 50 kN**

Now indicate that we want to compute the **Normal Stress, Strain** and **Displacement** in the **X Direction**.

20.   **Solution > Stress > Normal > Orientation > X Axis** (Same for strain and displacement)

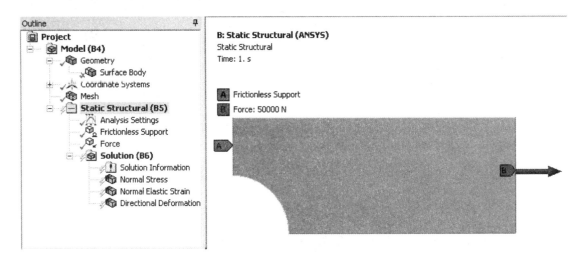

Figure 8-18 All environment conditions.

21.   **Solution > Solve** ⟋ Solve

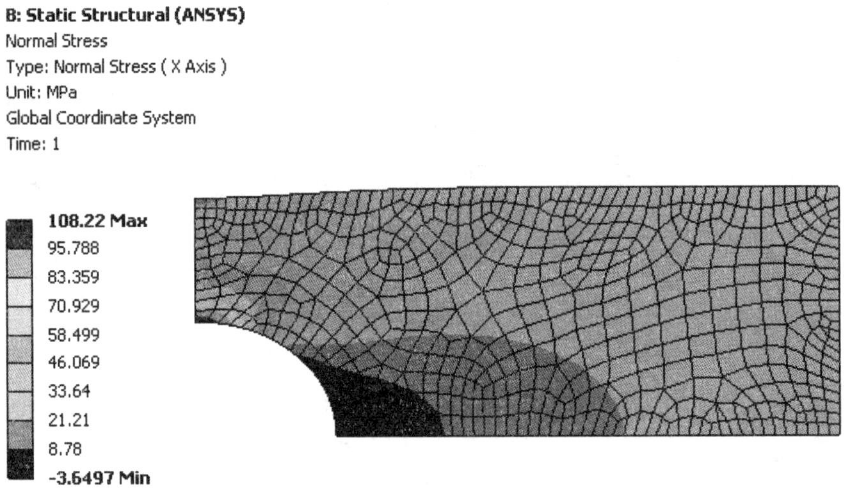

Figure 8-19 Normal stress in X direction.

The maximum value of the normal stress in the X direction is **108 MPa**, which is within 1 per cent of our previously computed and theoretical estimates in Chapter 4. The maximum stress and strain are well within elastic behavior limits.

B: Static Structural (ANSYS)
Normal Elastic Strain
Type: Normal Elastic Strain (X Axis)
Unit: mm/mm
Global Coordinate System
Time: 1

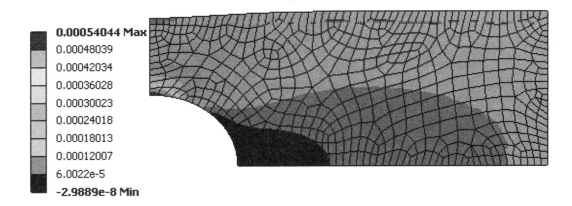

Figure 8-20 Normal strain in X direction.

B: Static Structural (ANSYS)
Directional Deformation
Type: Directional Deformation (X Axis)
Unit: mm
Global Coordinate System
Time: 1

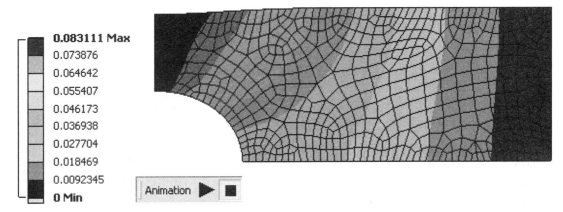

Figure 8-21 Deformation in X direction.

22.   Use the **Animation Option** to check the behavior. **Save your work.**

8-4   TUTORIAL 8B – PRESSURE VESSEL

Problems that are axisymmetric in nature can be solved with two-dimensional models using the ANSYS built-in analysis methods that **automatically incorporate** the **'hoop'** direction **stress** in the analysis of the 2D model. This tutorial revisits the pressure vessel problem we solved in Chapter 5. The process is very similar to that employed in T8A.

We need a **surface model** of the pressure vessel cross section. It is important to note that the 2D model **must be** drawn in the **X-Y Plane** and the **Y-axis must be** the axis of **symmetry**. We describe two ways to do this.

DESGIN MODELER

1. **Start ANSYS Workbench DesignModeler**

2. **Open the DM file for the pressure vessel from Chapter 5** and **select the sketch used to create the solid model by revolving.**

3. **Concept > Surfaces From Sketches**

Figure 8-22 Surface model (right) derived from the DM sketch.

USING ANOTHER SOLID MODELER

4. Use an **Alternate Solid Modeler** to create the **cross section of the pressure vessel** and **extrude** it an arbitrary amount **symmetrically** from a **sketch** in the **XY plane**.

Figure 8-23 Extruded section model.

5. **Attach to Active CAD Geometry** or **Import External Geometry File to bring the extrusion into DesignModeler**

6. **Tools > Mid-Surface**

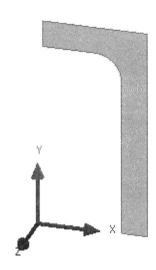

Figure 8-24 Mid-Surface.

BACK TO AXISYMMETRIC EXAMPLE - Proceed as in Tutorial 8A to set up a 2 dimensional analysis.

7. On the **Schematic** page, **Select Geometry cell A2,** then **View > Properties**

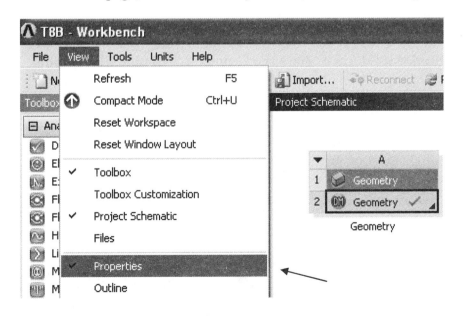

Figure 8-25 View Geometry Properties.

In the Project screen select Advanced Geometry Options.

8.   Advanced Geometry Options > Analysis Type > 2-D (See the next figure.)

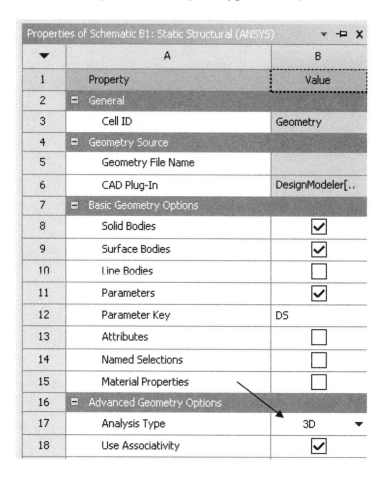

Figure 8-26 Change 3D to 2D.

9.   Add Static Structural > Share the Geometry > Double Click Model

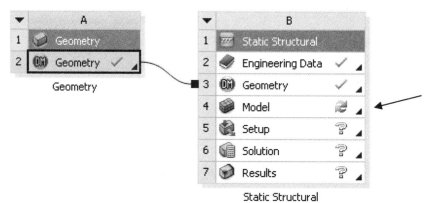

Figure 8-27 Share geometry.

10. Select **Geometry > Details of "Geometry" > 2D Behavior > Axisymmetric**

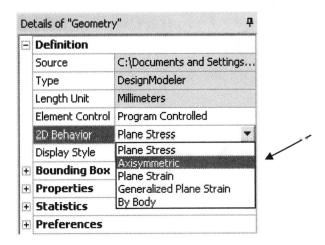

Figure 8-28 Select an axisymmetric model.

11. **Check the units**

12. **Environment > Supports > Displacement**

13. Click on the **Edge Selection Filter** 🖽.

14. Select the **Bottom Edge > Apply**

15. **Y Component > 0 mm** (Notice that only X and Y displacements are available.) The X Component is left Free. (The cylinder expands in the radial direction.)

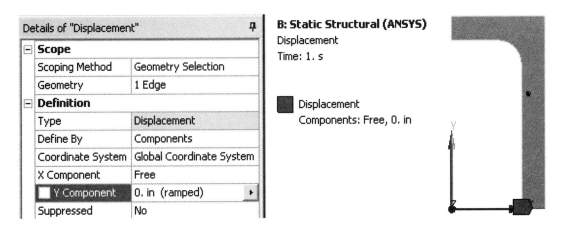

Figure 8-29 Displacement boundary condition.

The upper left edge of the sketch is on the **axis of symmetry** and **requires no displacement constraint**. Apply the internal pressure next.

16.   **Environment > Loads > Pressure > Cntl select the inside edge segments > Apply > Pressure Magnitude > 35 MPa**

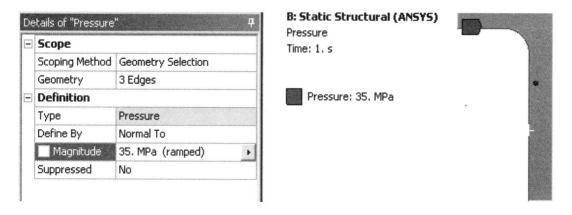

Figure 8-30 Pressure loading.

17.   Add solution item **Stress > Equivalent Stress (von Mises) > Solve** ⌐⁵ Solve

The following figure shows the von Mises stress distribution for the default coarse mesh and for a mesh using the medium relevance center setting. The second mesh maximum stress value compares well with the results calculated in Chapter 5. If anything, the contour curves for this simpler model are smoother at the maximum stress region, and we would expect the computed maximum equivalent stress (205 MPa) to be more accurate than that of Chapter 5 (207 MPa) where the coarseness of the mesh produced more jagged contour plots. But you see that the two values are only about 1.5 per cent different.

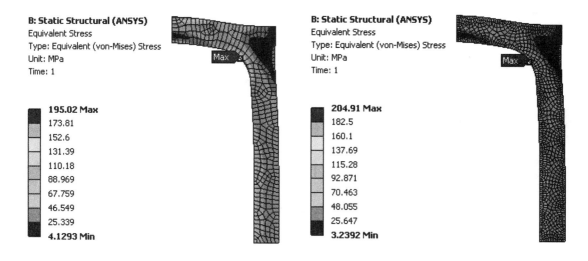

Figure 8-31 von Mises stress distribution.

If we add **Normal Stress** and **Directional Displacement** solution items we can make a complete comparison of this model with the theoretical solution at the base as before. The normal stress in the **Z-direction** is the **hoop stress** for this axisymmetric problem. The results shown in the table below are virtually identical with those shown in Chapter 5.

Results

	Theoretical	Workbench	Error, per cent
Hoop Stress (Sx), MPa	125	127	1.9
Axial Stress (Sy), MPa	45	46.5	3.3
Radial Stress (Sz), MPa	-35	-34.9	0.3
Radial Deflection, mm	0.0458	0.0465	1.5

Tutorial T8B has 2D axisymmetric modeling as its focus while the next tutorial is concerned with **3D surface modeling** using plate (shell) elements. **Save your work.**

8-5 TUTORIAL 8C – BRACKET

The **objective** of this tutorial is to compute the **stress** and **deflection** response of the steel bracket that was analyzed in Chapter 5. See the figure below. The bracket is 100 mm high, 50 mm deep, 60 mm in width, and has a 10 mm thickness. It has a 30 mm diameter hole located 70 mm from its base plane. The fillet radii are 10 and 20 mm, and the 10 mm mounting bolt holes are located 15 mm from the front and side edges. The bearing is subjected to load components 5500 N in the X direction, 3500 N in Y, and 1700 N in Z. The base of the bracket is fixed against all motion.

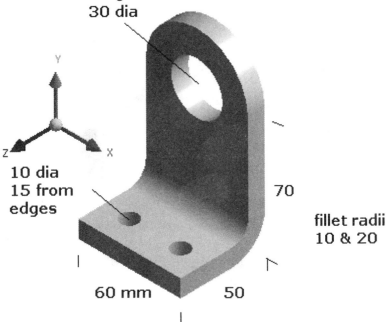

Figure 8-32 Bracket.

We will start with the solid model of the bracket and create an equivalent **surface model**.

1.   Start **ANSYS Workbench DesignModeler** and **create** or **attach** the bracket **solid model geometry**.

We want to create a **3D surface** corresponding to the **middle surface** of the bracket.

2.   **Tools > Midsurface**

Figure 8-33 Mid-Surface tool.

3.   **Details of MidSurf1 > Face Pairs**

4.   Use **Cntl Select** to sequentially pick **all** the **front** and **corresponding back** face pairs on the bracket model > **Apply**.

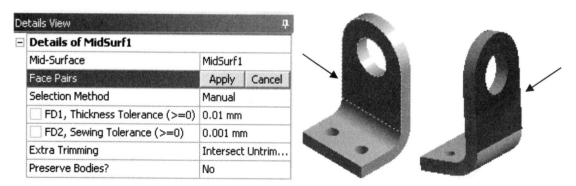

Figure 8-34 Mid-Surface face pairs.

5.   **Generate**   ⌇ Generate   To create the surface.

Notice that this is a **three-dimensional surface model**. No change in dimensionality is required as in T8A and T8B.

6.   Make sure the thickness = 10 mm

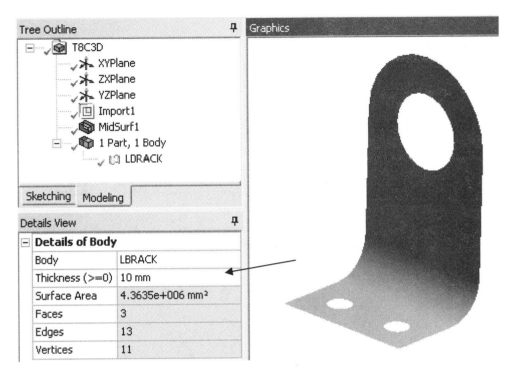

Figure 8-35 3D surface model of bracket.

(**Note:** You will generally have better results if you use a **STEP** file instead of an **IGES** file to bring geometry into DesignModeler when using a neutral file format.)

7.   Project Schematic > Add Static Structural > Share the Geometry > Double Click Engineering Data

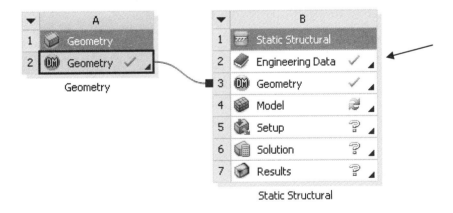

Figure 8-36 Engineering Data.

Be sure **View > Properties & Outline** and **Engineering Data Sources** are on.

8.   **Select General Materials > Aluminum Alloy > Click** 🔲 **to add this material to the project.**

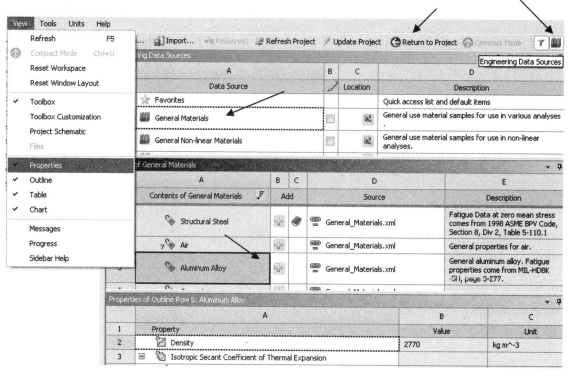

Figure 8-37 Add Aluminum Alloy.

9.   After adding Aluminum, **Return to Project** 🔙 Return to Project

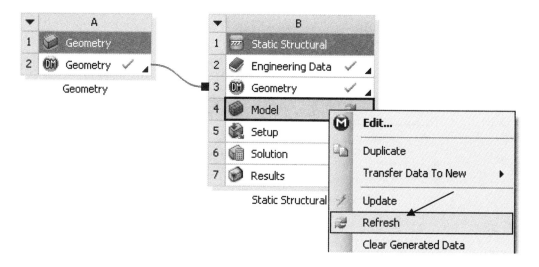

Figure 8-38 Right Click **Model > Refresh** the model.

10. **Double Click Model**

11. **Environment > Supports > Fixed Support** (Set selection filter to surface.)

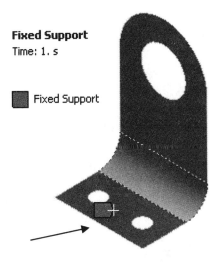

Figure 8-39 Apply Fixed support to the surface.

12. **Environment > Loads > Force**

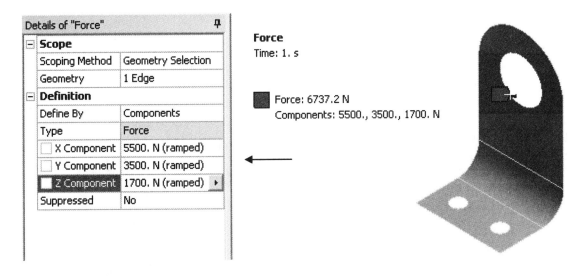

Figure 8-40 Apply force components to the large circular hole.

13. **Solution > Stress > Equivalent Stress (von Mises)**

14. **Solution > Stress > Error**

15. **Solution > Deformation > Total**

16. **Solution > Solve** ⚡ Solve

The computed von Mises stress is shown in the next figure.

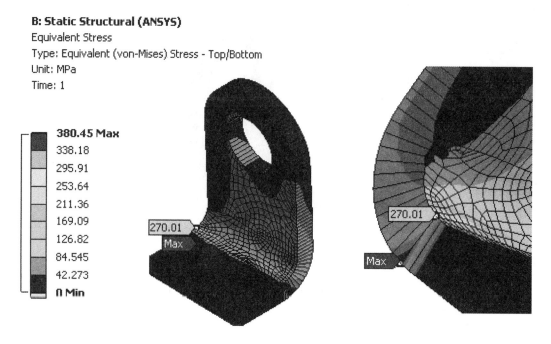

Figure 8-41 von Mises stresses.

The von Mises stress value on the inside of the fillet (270 MPa) compares reasonably well with the result we calculated in Chapter 5 even though this part is a little thick in relation to its 'length' to be typical of plate geometry. Note that the mesh is displayed as a **three-dimensional mesh** even though the model is really a surface model. Bending stresses vary linearly from the middle surface in a plate model, so the surface mesh is extended as a prism on both sides of the mid-surface for display purposes.

The maximum **total displacement** is computed to be 1.15 mm which is about 16 per cent smaller than the 1.37 we calculated with the solid model in Chapter 5. This is due to the difference in the solid and plate modeling.

Figure 8-42 Total deformation.

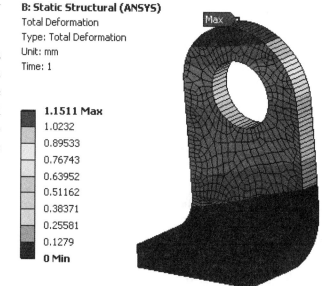

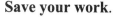**Save your work**.

17. **Workbench > File > Save (or Save As) > T8C**

This concludes the three-dimensional surface modeling exercise with plate (shell) elements. There are many objects where plate modeling is an appropriate choice for analysis, particularly when bending of thin parts dominates the behavior. See Tutorial T9B.

8-6 TUTORIAL 8D – LINE-BODY MODEL

In the final tutorial of this chapter we attach the line-body model of Chapter 3 Tutorial T3D and perform structural analysis using ANSYS beam elements. The object is to determine the displacement and stress response to a horizontal load applied to the structure.

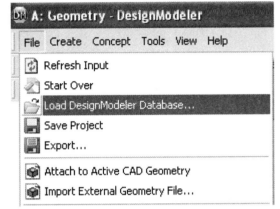

1. **Start ANSYS Workbench DesignModeler** and **create** or **attach the T3D tutorial geometry**.

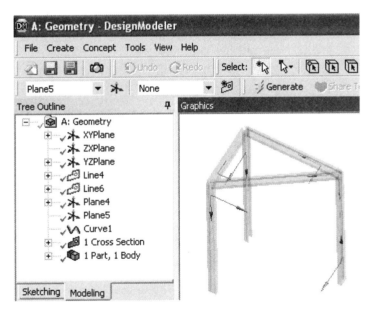

Figure 8-43 Beam model from DesignModeler Database.

2. **Project Schematic > Add Static Structural > Right Click Geometry > View > Properties** > add **Line Bodies in Properties array**

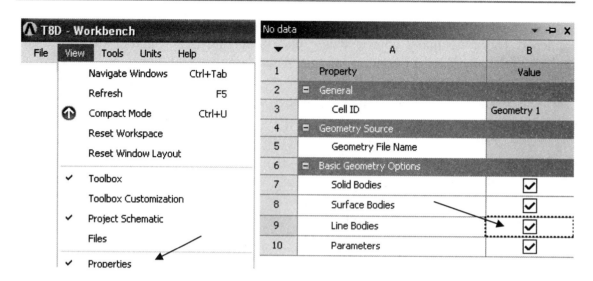

Figure 8-44 Add Line Bodies option.

3.   **Check the units** and make sure you are working in **inch-lbf-sec units**.

4.   **Double Click Model > Select Wireframe**

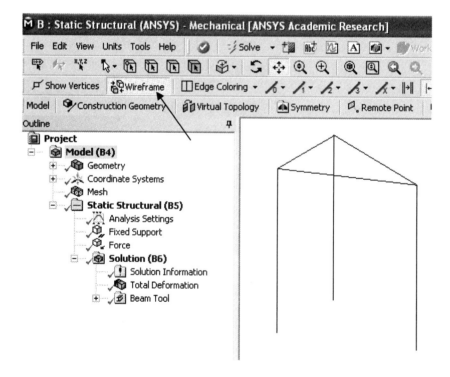

Figure 8-45 Line bodies model in Mechanical.

5.   **Right Click Mesh > Generate Mesh**

If the channel leg orientation of any edge is incorrect as shown in the figure on the left below, return to DesignModeler and fix it. (See Chapter 3.)

6. **DesignModeler > Edge Selection Filter > Select Edge > Change the Reverse Orientation Flag (Yes** to **No** or **No** to **Yes)**

7. **Project >** Update **Model** using parameter values and geometry from **Tutorial T3D**.

8. **Simulation > Right Click Mesh > Preview Mesh**

Figure 8-46 Default mesh and reversed section orientation.

9. **Environment > Supports > Fixed Support**

10. **Ctrl Select the three column base points > Details of "Fixed Support" > Geometry > Apply** (Set selection filter to point.)

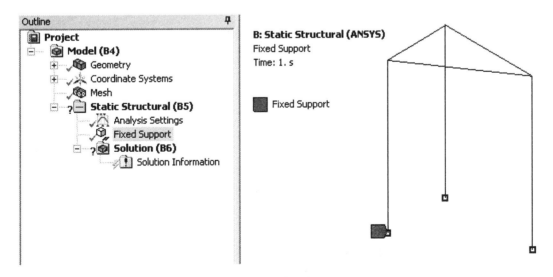

Figure 8-47 Fixed supports.

Also apply a horizontal loading of **5,000 lbf** in the **Z Direction** to the upper vertex that lies in the XY Plane.

11.   Environment > Loads > Force

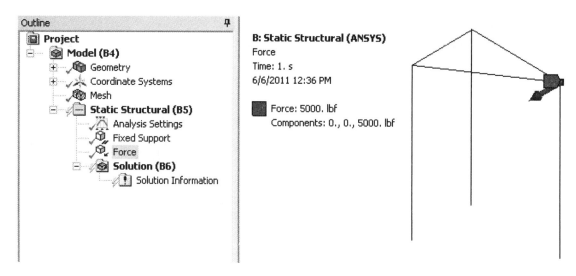

Figure 8-48 Applied loading.

12.   Solution > Deformation Directional > Z Axis

13.   Solution > Tools > Beam Tool > Solve

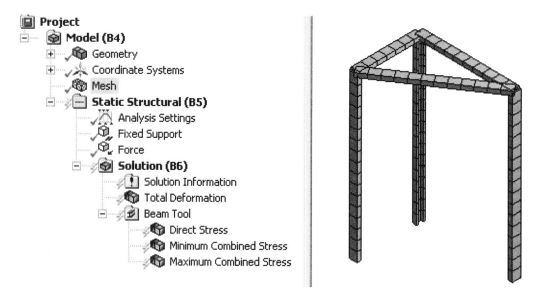

Figure 8-49 Add the Beam tool.

The **beam tool** uses the cross section properties and orientation to compute the **direct (axial) stress** as well as the **minimum and maximum stresses** over the cross section that result when the **direct stress is combined with the bending stress**.

We can display all four of these results at once by selecting multiple viewports. Select the four viewports option using the top row icon shown. Select a viewport then select an item to display.

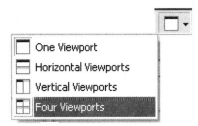

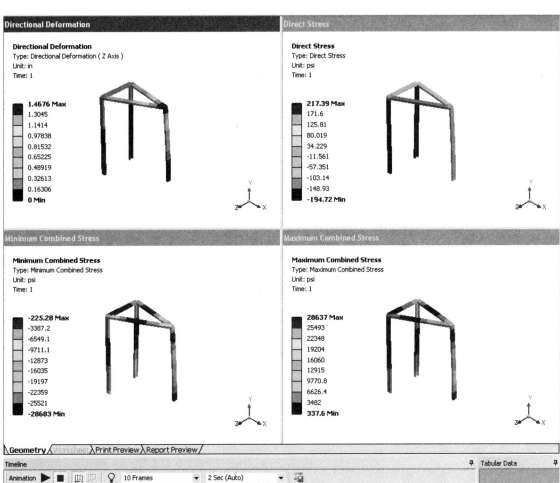

Figure 8-50 Outputs shown in four viewports.

Visualize the deformation and stress progression during loading by selecting the **animation option** at the bottom of the screen. Control the animation using the icons

Animation ▶ ■

14. **Save your work.**

8-7 SUMMARY

The tutorials of Chapter 8 introduce the use of surface models in ANSYS Workbench Mechanical and present results that agree with those we calculated previously using three-dimensional solid models. There are many engineering situations in which surface model development proves to be a cost effective and convenient analysis method when compared with comparable three-dimensional, solid modeling analysis approaches. For example, Tutorials T7A and T7C could be solved using 2D models. This chapter concludes by illustrating the use of line body models for those situations where beam elements are an appropriate option for analysis.

8-8 PROBLEMS

8-1 Formulate and solve Tutorial T4B as a surface model problem; be sure to include the interior corner fillet radius. Compare your results with those calculated in Chapter 4.

8-2 Compute the results shown in the table at the end of Tutorial T8B in this chapter.

8-3 Formulate and solve Tutorial T7C as a plane stress surface model problem.

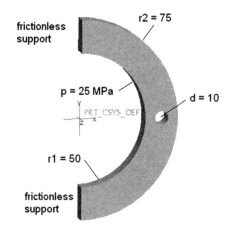

Figure 8-3

8-4 Formulate and solve Tutorial T8D as solid model problem instead of a beam element model.

8-5 Determine the magnitude and location of the **maximum von Mises stress** and the magnitude and location of the **maximum displacement** of the structural steel part (dimensions are in **mm**) shown under the following conditions.

a. Has a **thickness of 15 mm** and is a state of **plane stress**.

Figure 8-5 a.

b. It is a **long** object in a state of **plane strain**. Same loading as **a.** (see next figure)

c. It is **axisymmetric** (a sphere with an internal cavity).

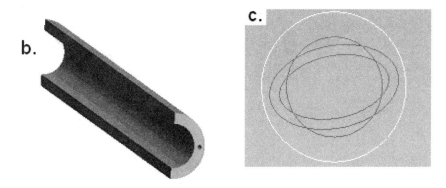

8-6 Solve problems 4-1 through 4-7 as problems in plane stress.

8-7 Solve problem 4-8 as a problem in plane strain.

Chapter 9

Natural Frequencies
&
Buckling Loads

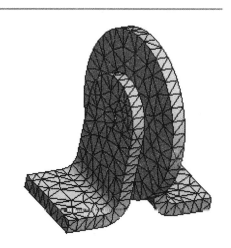

9-1   OVERVIEW

In this Chapter we discuss use of ANSYS Workbench to determine the natural frequencies and normal modes of structural parts and systems. The determination of buckling load estimates for structural systems is also covered. In particular we illustrate the determination of

- ◆ Natural frequencies

- ◆ Corresponding mode shapes

- ◆ Buckling load estimates

9-2   INTRODUCTION

Natural frequencies of systems are those frequencies at which resonant response occurs under the right excitation conditions. Knowledge of these critical dynamic frequencies is an essential step in the design or evaluation of a system subjected to dynamic loadings.

Static loads too can produce instabilities given the particular combination of geometry and loading. Buckling of a long slender bar in axial compression is a common example.

This chapter presents tutorials that illustrate the use of the ANSYS Simulation software suite to address both of these problems.

9-3   TUTORIAL 9A – SIMPLY SUPPORTED BEAM FREQUENCIES

In this first tutorial we compute the natural frequencies of vibration of a long slender bar that has pinned supports at both ends.

Consider a **steel** bar **0.5 inch in thickness, 1.0 inch high**, and **25 inches in length** between **0.5 inch diameter pins.** See the figure below. Calculate the first **four bending frequencies** of this beam.

The first step is to create the solid model of the beam. Open ANSYS DesignModeler or other parametric modeling system and develop the beam model using the dimensions indicated. We will follow the Simulation Wizard outline.

Figure 9-1 Beam.

1.   **Start ANSYS Workbench DesignModeler; create** or **attach the beam geometry.** Check the units.

2.   **Add Modal Analysis to the Project**

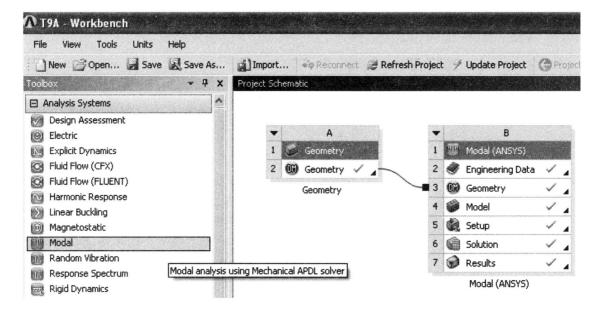

Figure 9-2 Add Modal Analysis to the Project.

Add the link to share the geometry.

3.   **Double Click Model** in **cell B4** to start **ANSYS Mechanical**

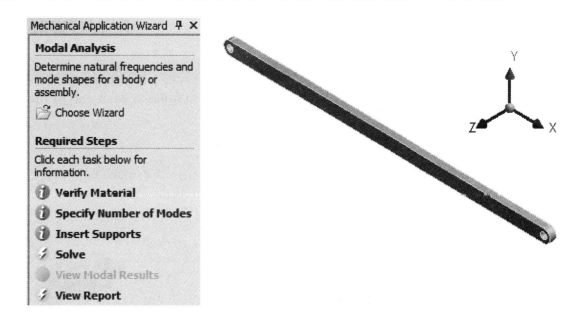

Figure 9-3 Modal analysis requirements.

4. **Verify Material** (Use the default material properties for steel.)

5. **Modal > Analysis Settings > Max Modes to Find > 4**

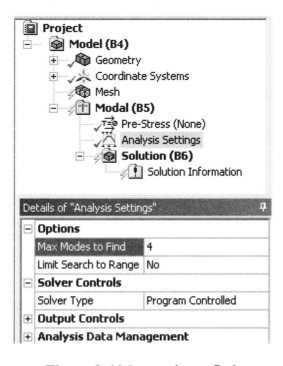

Figure 9-4 Max modes to find.

6. **Insert Supports** ✔ Insert Supports

7. **Environment > Supports > Cylindrical Support**

8. **Ctrl Select the Inside surfaces** of the **cylindrical holes** at **each end of the beam.**

9. **Radial > Fixed**

10. **Axial > Fixed**

11. **Tangential > Free** (See the next figure.)

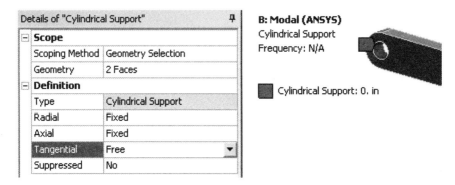

Figure 9-5 Cylindrical support conditions.

Set the mesh density by specifying an **element size** of **0.5 inch**.

12. **Mesh > Advanced > Element Size > 0.5 in >Generate Mesh**

Insert a deformation object in the Solution branch.

13. **Solution > Deformation > Total**

14. **Solve** ⚡ Solve

15. **Select Total Deformation to View Results** ✔ View Modal Results

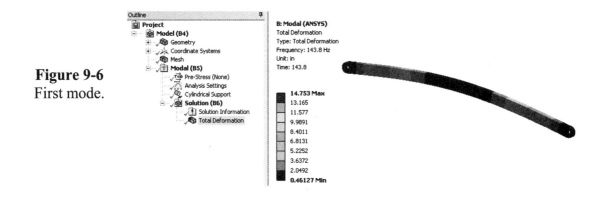

Figure 9-6
First mode.

The **first natural frequency** is computed to be **143.8 Hz**, and the first mode shows the mid point deflecting the greatest amount. The plot deformation scale (14.7 max in this case) is **arbitrary**. The mode shape plot just shows the shape of the beam if it were forced to vibrate at this 'natural' frequency.

16. To better visualize the mode, select the **front view** and click the **Animation tab** from the options at the bottom of the screen.

Figure 9-7 First mode.

17. **Rename the Total Deformation object 'Mode 1'**

Insert a second deformation object in the Solution branch and name it **'Mode 2'**.

18. **Solution > Deformation > Total; Rename 'Mode 2'**

In 'Details', change from mode 1 to mode 2 then evaluate the results.

19. **Details of 'Mode 2'** > Use the arrows to change **Mode** from **1** to **2**

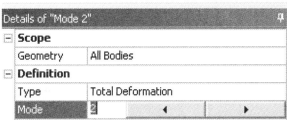

Figure 9-8 Change to second mode.

20. **Solution > Mode 2 > Right click > Evaluate All Results** (Retrieve This Result.)

Figure 9-9 Evaluate second mode.

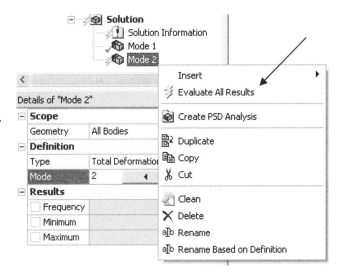

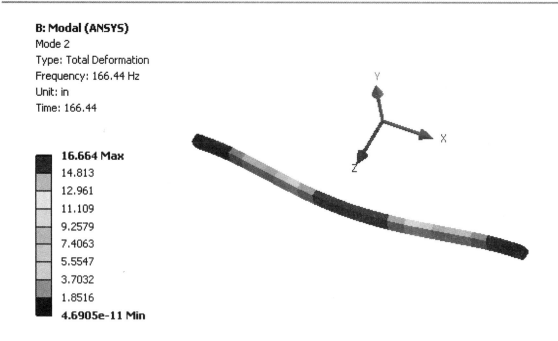

Figure 9-10 Second mode.

Examine Mode 2 from the top. (**Right click > View > Top**)

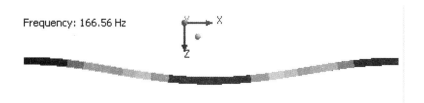

Figure 9-11 Second mode.

Add deformation objects and evaluate frequency results for modes 3 and 4.

Note that the second and third modes are at frequencies of **166 Hz** and **458 Hz** and both are **out-plane modes**. They occur in the **XZ Plane** instead of the **XY Plane**.

Notice also that these modes have **fixed-fixed** type **end conditions**; that is, there is no displacement or slope at the ends.

The fourth mode has a frequency of **571 Hz** and is a **pinned-pinned bending** mode in the **XY Plane**.

The four modes are shown together in a four viewport view below. Be sure to use the **animation** options to visualize each mode of vibration.

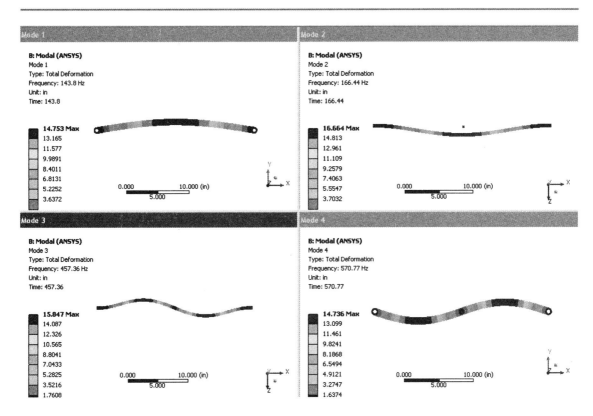

Figure 9-12 First four modes.

Although the modeling here is with three-dimensional solid elements as shown in the figures above, the results can be checked using **engineering beam theory** together with appropriate cross section and boundary conditions. We need the area moment of inertia for bending. (I = w h³/12):

Pinned-pinned case, cross section base w = 0.5, height h = 1.0, modes 1 and 4: 144 Hz and 576 Hz.

Fixed-fixed case, cross section base w = 1.0, height h = 0.5, modes 2 and 3: 163 Hz and 450 Hz.

The table below summarizes these results.

Frequency Results

Mode	Workbench (Hz)	Beam Theory (Hz)
1	144	144 (pinned)
2	166	163 (fixed)
3	457	450 (fixed)
4	571	576 (pinned)

The frequency differences are insignificantly small and are caused to some extent in modes 2 and 3 by the fact that the 3D cylindrical supports are not quite correctly modeled by fixed-fixed beam end conditions. A refined mesh produces only small **changes in the computed frequencies, however we find that the default** mesh is too coarse to give meaningful results; try it to see. That is why you were asked to refine the mesh at the outset. In more complex problems convergence with mesh refinement is an obvious characteristic of the modeling/solution process.

9-4   TUTORIAL 9B – NATURAL FREQUENCIES OF A CHIME

Consider the wind chime shown in the figure to the right. We will use the frequency finder simulation tool to determine the natural frequencies of one of its component tubes.

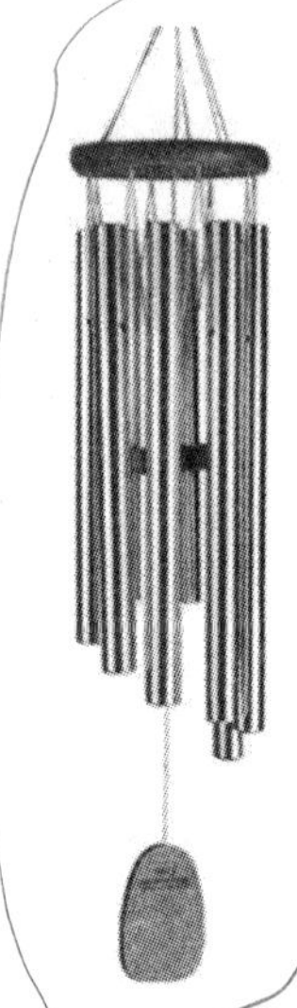

Figure 9-13 Wind chimes.

The shortest chime in the group is used in this tutorial; it is an **aluminum** tube **10.5 inches** in length with an **outer diameter** of $29/32 = $ **0.90625 inch**, and a **wall thickness** of $1/16 = $ **0.0625 inch**.

1.   Use DesignModeler or another **CAD system** to **create** a **solid model of the tube** described above. **Open** this model in **DesignModeler**. **Workbench > DesignModeler**

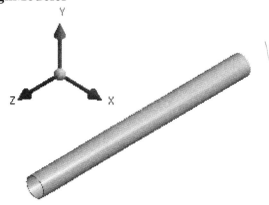

Figure 9-14 10.5 inch tube.

Because the tube very long in comparison to its thickness, we will create a **midsurface model** from this solid to use in the analysis.

2.   **DesignModeler > Tools > Mid-Surface > Click the Outer Surface > Ctrl Click the Inner Surface > Apply**

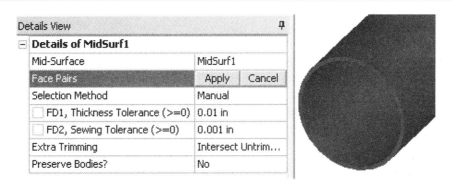

Figure 9-15 Surface pairs selection.

3. **Generate** Generate

4. **Surface Body > Thickness > 0.0625**

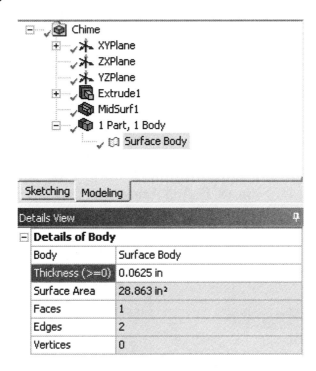

Figure 9-16 Surface body thickness.

Add the **Modal Analysis** module to the Project and check to see that the **Units** are set correctly.

5. **Workbench >Dbl Click** or **Drag Modal Analysis** to **Add** it to the **Schematic: Units >** inches, etc

6. **Dbl Click > Engineering Data** to add **Aluminum Alloy** to the **Project materials**

7.   General Materials > Aluminum Alloy. ⊞

▼	A	B	C	D
1	Data Source	⟋	Location	Description
2	📖 Engineering Data		B2	Contents filtered for Modal (ANSYS).
3	📚 General Materials	☐	🔍	General use material samples for use in various analyses.
4	📚 General Non-linear Materials	☐	🔍	General use material samples for use in non-linear analyses.
5	📚 Explicit Materials	☐	🔍	Material samples for use in an explicit anaylsis.
6	📚 Hyperelastic Materials	☐	🔍	Material stress-strain data samples for curve fitting.
7	📚 Magnetic B-H Curves	☐	🔍	B-H Curve samples specific for use in a magnetic analysis.
8	☆ Favorites			Quick access list and default items
*	Click here to add a new library		...	

Outline of General Materials

▼	A	B	C	D	E
1	Contents of General Materials ⬆	Add		S..	Description
2	⊟ Material				
3	🔖 Air	⊞		⊜	General properties for air.
4	🔖 Aluminum Alloy	⊞	📖	⊜	General aluminum alloy. Fatigue properties come from MIL-HDBK-5H, page 3-277.
5	🔖 Concrete	⊞		⊜	

Figure 9-17 Add Aluminum Alloy.

8.   Return to Project ⬅ Return to Project

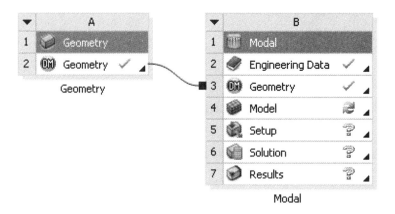

Figure 9-18 Refresh the model.

9.   Double Click Model. Change part **Material** to **Aluminum.**

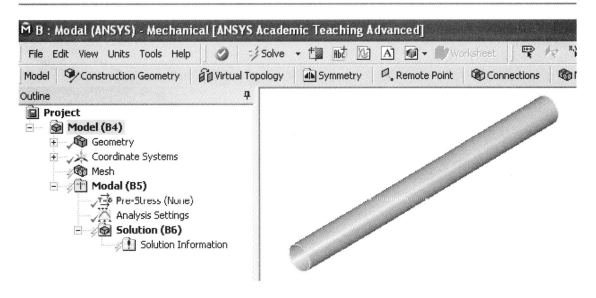

Figure 9-19 Tube surface.

10.   Right click Mesh > Generate Mesh

Since the default mesh is not very uniform, we will replace it with a **mapped mesh** in which a regular pattern of rectangles is mapped onto the surface.

11.   Right click Mesh > Insert > Mapped Face Meshing > Select the Surface > Apply

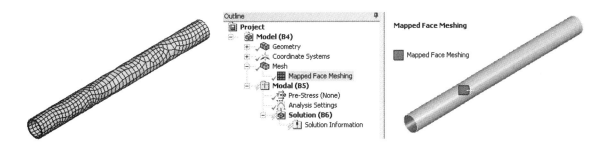

Figure 9-20 Meshing options.

12.   Right click > Generate Mesh

Note that the mapped mesh process produces a nice regular mesh of 1122 **shell elements**.

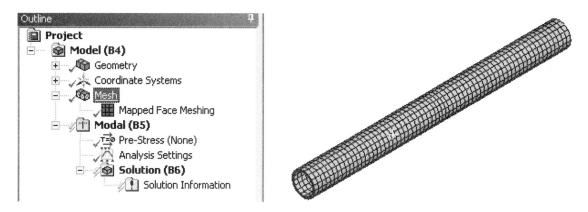

Figure 9-21 Mapped mesh.

13.   New Analysis > Modal

When the tube is installed in the chime it is essentially in a **free motion condition** supported only by the cord from which it is suspended. For this reason we will **not apply any displacement boundary conditions** and will calculate the frequencies in a **free-free** condition as we would do for an aircraft or spacecraft in flight.

Because of the free-free boundary conditions, there will be **six zero-frequency, rigid body modes** corresponding to the six rigid body degrees of freedom. The chime sound is produced by the **elastic vibration modes**, so we set the number of modes to be calculated to 9 anticipating that the sounds we are interested in are contained in **modes 7 – 9** and above.

14.   Details of Analysis Settings > Max Modes to Find > 9

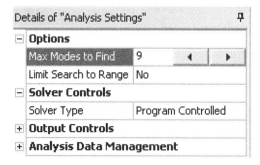

Figure 9-22 Max modes to find.

15.   Solve ⚡ Solve

The results show that the **first six modes** have **a zero or near zero frequency** and the **seventh mode** has a frequency of **1.8 kHz**. Because of symmetry, the eighth mode is the same as the seventh but in a different plane.

A good way to better understand the behavior is to use **animation** 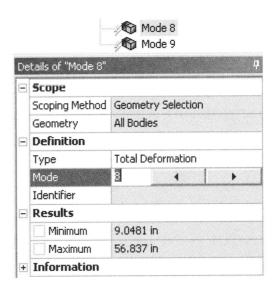 to view the **mode shape**. It also helps to display the undeformed model. First insert **Total Deformation** into the list of Solution items to be computed. Rename them Mode 1, Mode 2, etc. In addition you need to set the Mode number to correspond with the Shape number as we did in the previous example.

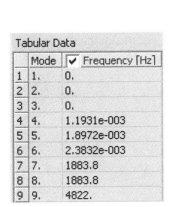

Figure 9-23 Frequency data.

Figure 9-24 Set Total Deformation Index.

16. Show Undeformed Model

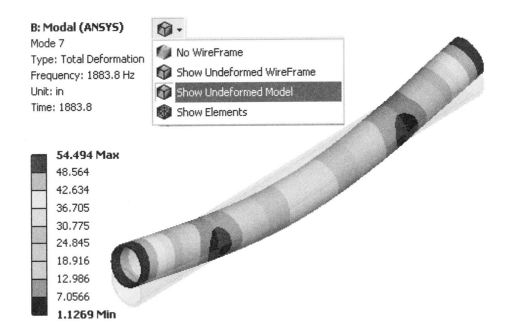

Figure 9-25 Seventh mode.

The figure shows the seventh mode which is an **elastic bending mode at 1.8 kHz**. The dark regions on the sides are **nodes**, regions of no displacement. Take a look at the photo of the chime and you note that this is the point where the holes are drilled for the support chord since a constraint here does not influence this vibration mode. Note also that the striker hits each chime near the middle so as to excite this mode of bending.

Note again that the mode deformation plot scale is **arbitrary**. The plot just shows the shape of the chime if it were forced to vibrate at this 'natural' frequency.

We would have gotten the same results if we had used a **solid model of brick elements** instead a surface model for this problem, but the calculation time is much longer owing to the large number of elements in the mesh required to obtain accurate results.

(If you have access to a chime, have a computer microphone and frequency analysis software installed, see www.relisoft.com, you can verify this type of analysis experimentally.)

9-5   TUTORIAL 9C – NATURAL FREQUENCIES OF AN ASSEMBLY

In this tutorial we determine the natural frequencies of an assembly of component parts. First create a **110 mm diameter rotor** that is **10 mm thick** and has an integral **axle 15 mm** in **diameter** and **42 mm** in over all **length**. A **20 mm diameter boss** protrudes **5 mm** on each side of the rotor.

Modify the bracket from Chapter 5 by eliminating the base holes and reducing the size of the bore to fit the 15 mm shaft. Create the assembly shown below.

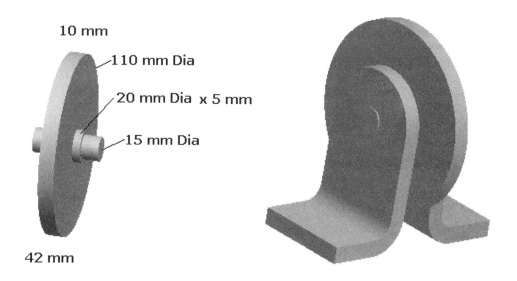

Figure 9-26 Rotor assembly.

1.   **Start ANSYS Workbench. Use DesignModeler** to **attach the assembly.** Check that the units are set for mm. We will use the default **structural steel** material.

A contact region is defined between the axle and the bore as well as the inside face of the bracket and the rotor boss on each side of the rotor. Define these contacts to be **No Separation**. This allows small relative motion between the surfaces so the disk can rotate on its shaft.

To better visualize the contact regions, use the wireframe display option.

2.   **View > Wireframe**

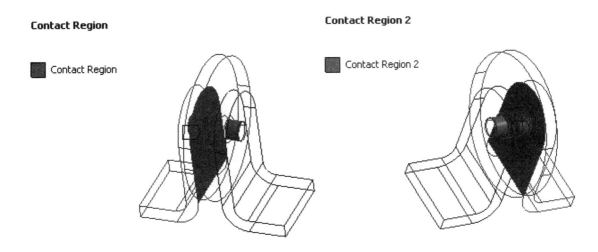

Figure 9-27 Rotor assembly.

3.   **Contact > Contact Region > Type > No Separation**

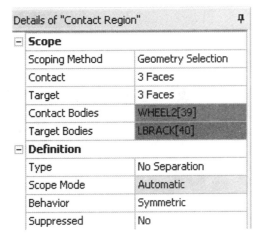

Figure 9-28 No Separation contacts.

Set the default mesh size

4.   **Mesh > Details of Mesh > Advanced > Element Size; Enter 0, Press Return.**

5.   **New Analysis > Modal**

6.   **Environment > Supports > Fixed Support > Ctrl click base, two faces > Apply** (Fix the base from motion.)

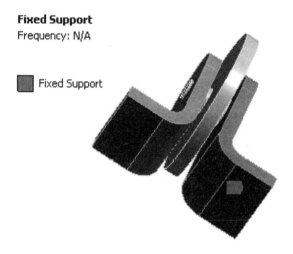

Figure 9-29 Fixed supports.

7.   **Details of Analysis Settings > Max Modes to Find > 6** (Default)

8.   **Solve** Solve

The default mesh of 1578 elements is shown below together with a display of the first two modes computed.

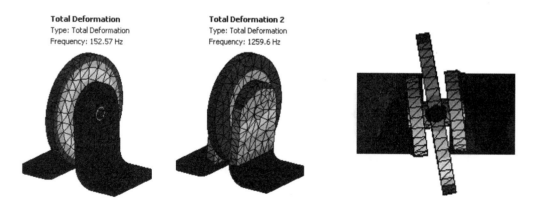

Figure 9-30 First two modes and top view of Mode 2.

Use the **animation** option to examine each mode in turn. The table below summarizes the results. Zoom in to a close view of the pin and bracket connection to observe the relative motion during animation for modes 1 and 4.

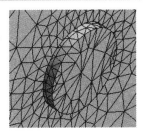

Frequency Results

Mode	Frequency (Hz)	Description
1	153	Rigid body rotation of rotor
2	1116	Twisting about vertical axis
3	1175	Side-to-side
4	1637	Fore-aft bracket bending
5	1793	Twisting about horizontal axis
6	3752	Rotor flexure about diameter

The frequency for the first mode of the assembly was calculated to be 152 Hz whereas we see from the mode shape animation that this mode is really a rigid body mode and should be zero. Refine the mesh of the assembly model in order to define contact conditions more accurately.

9. **Mesh > Details of Mesh > Sizing > Relevance Center > Fine**

10. **Right Click Mesh > Insert > Refinement Select the Pin component surface**

11. **Repeat for the Upright bracket holes.**

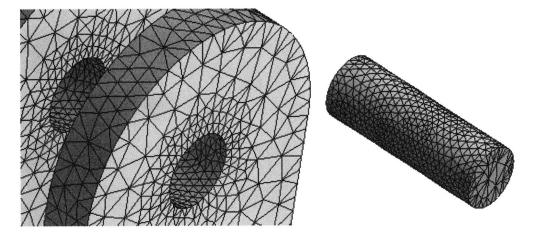

Figure 9-31 Refined meshes.

The new model has over 22,000 elements and almost 40,000 nodes.

12. **Solve** Solve

The computed frequencies are shown below.

Frequency Results (Refined Mesh)

Mode	Frequency (Hz)	Description
1	12.5	Rigid body
2	1067	Rotor twisting about vertical axis
3	1130	Side-to-side bending of brackets
4	1558	Fore-aft bracket bending
5	1659	Rotor twisting about horizontal axis
6	3673	Rotor flexure about a diameter

We see from these results that the both first mode (a rigid body mode) as well as the higher elastic modes are measurably influenced by the quality of the mesh. The contact description, as well as the distribution of both mass and stiffness, strongly depends upon the mesh and thus the frequencies calculated are dependent upon the mesh.

Refine the mesh further as your computer hardware and time budget permit and you may see a point at which the results **converge** to values somewhat smaller than those shown. The calculated Mode 1 frequency is not zero but it's ten times smaller than our first estimate and almost 100 smaller than Mode 2, the first elastic frequency.

13.   Save your work

9-6   BUCKLING LOADS

ANSYS Simulation provides tools for computing buckling estimates of elastic structures. We start by considering two problems that can readily be checked, a fixed-free column and a pinned-pinned column.

9-7   TUTORIAL 9D – FIXED-FREE COLUMN (FLAGPOLE)

First use DesignModeler or another solid modeler to create geometry for a solid bar **0.5 x 1 x 25 inch**. See below.

Figure 9-32 25 x 1 x 0.5 inch solid.

1.   Start ANSYS Workbench. Use DesignModeler to create or **attach the column geometry.** Check the **units**. We will use the default **structural steel** material.

2. **Workbench Project > Double Click** or **Drag Static Structural** to add it to the **Project > Share the Geometry**

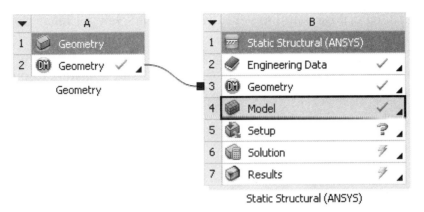

Figure 9-33 Insert Static Structural.

3. **Double Click Model** to start **ANSYS Mechanical**

4. **Mesh > Advanced > Element Size > 0.5 in >Generate Mesh**

Fix the left end completely.

5. **Environment > Supports > Fixed Support**

On the right end apply a **unit load of 1.0 lbf** in the **negative X Direction**. The computed buckling load will be a multiple of this unit load.

6. **Environment > Loads > Force > X Component > -1.0**

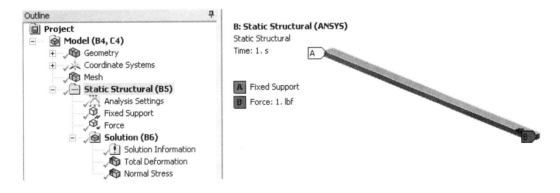

Figure 9-34 Boundary conditions and loading.

7. **Solution > Total Deformation & Normal Stress in X-Direction**

8.   **Solve** ⚡ Solve Find the deformation and stress

Next insert the **Linear Buckling** object.

9.   **Right Click** on **cell B6 Solution > Transfer Data** to **New > Linear Buckling** (See next figure)

This adds the Linear Buckling Analysis to the Project and transfers to model and data from the Static Structural Analysis including the solution results.

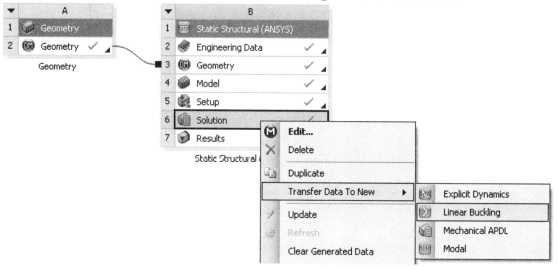

Figure 9-35 Transfer Data.

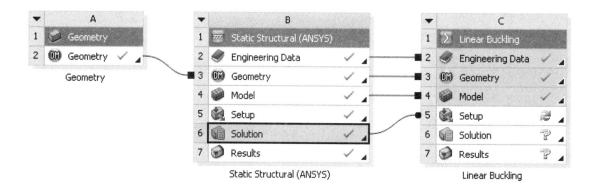

Figure 9-36 Linear Buckling.

9.   **Select ANSYS Mechanical** from list of **processes running** ⓜ B : Static Structural...

10.   Analysis Settings Max Modes to Find = 1 and **Insert > Total Deformation**

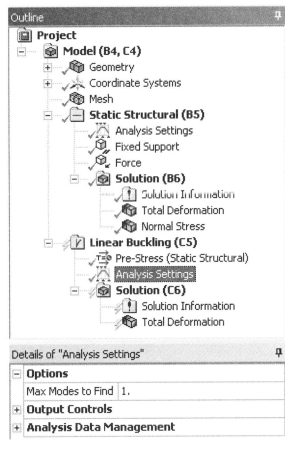

Figure 9-37 Model tree.

11.   Solve **Solve**   Find the Linear Elastic Buckling Load and the Deformed Shape.

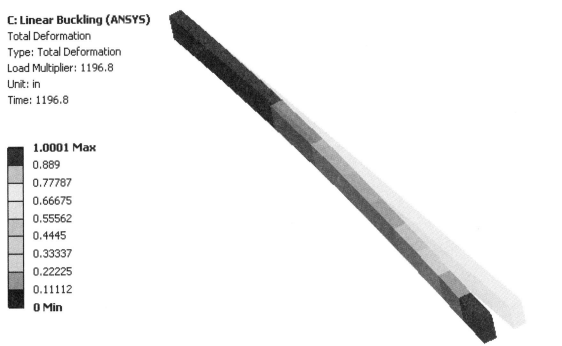

C: Linear Buckling (ANSYS)
Total Deformation
Type: Total Deformation
Load Multiplier: 1196.8
Unit: in
Time: 1196.8

1.0001 Max
0.889
0.77787
0.66675
0.55562
0.4445
0.33337
0.22225
0.11112
0 Min

Figure 9-38 XZ Plane buckling.

Rotate the view to something like what is shown above. **Animation** shows clearly that the deformation is in the **XZ Plane** (the direction of weaker flexural stiffness). The critical load multiplier is 1197. Since we applied a 1.0 lbf load, our buckling load is **1197 lbf.** If we use solid mechanics theory to compute the solution to this problem (cross section base $w = 1.0$, height $h = 0.5$) we get a comparable critical load of **1193 lbf.**

To see if the mesh is influencing the results, reduce the element size and solve again.

To get more information about the behavior of this geometry, elect to solve for an additional buckling mode.

8.   Linear Buckling > Analysis Settings > Max Modes to Find > 2

The second mode corresponds to buckling in the **XY Plane** with a load of about **4777 lbf.** This result also can be verified using column theory as before.

Why Static Structural Analysis + Linear Buckling Analysis? The static analysis performed before the buckling analysis is necessary in order to determine internal distribution of compressive stresses in the model. The structures in this example and the next are so simple it's obvious, but in more complex structures that distribution is not easy to see.

Save your work before moving to the next tutorial.

9-8   TUTORIAL 9E – BUCKLING OF A PINNED-PINNED COLUMN

We can use the geometry of Tutorial 9A to analyze buckling of a pinned-pinned column. The column is 0.5 x 1and 25 inches between the 0.5 inch holes on each end.

1.   Start ANSYS Workbench. Use DesignModeler to create or attach the beam geometry. Check the units.

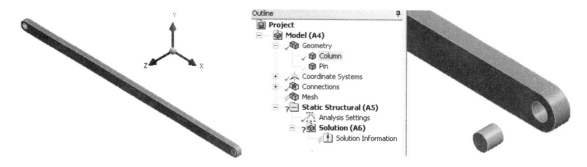

Figure 9-39 Pinned-pinned beam/column.

The column structural model requires the **freedom to move** along the **X Axis** in the direction of the applied 1 lbf load as discussed at the end of the previous tutorial. If we use a cylindrical support at both ends as before, the radial constraint will prevent this. A '**work around**' is to use a cylindrical pin on one end and load the column through the pin.

2.   **Use** DesignModeler or your other favorite solid modeler to create a **0.5 inch diameter pin** for the hole in the right end of the beam and **assemble the two components**.

We have not taken this approach in earlier tutorials, but Geometry can be directly accessed through the structural static analysis module.

3.   Start a new **Project,** insert the **Structural Static** analysis module and **double click Geometry.** This starts **DesignModeler. Open** the **pin-beam assembly** in DesignModeler.

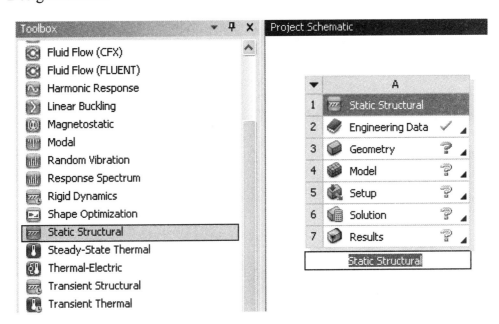

Figure 9-40 Pin contact with column.

Apply a **Cylindrical Support** to the left end of the column.

11.   **Environment > Supports > Cylindrical Support**

12.   **Ctrl Select the Inside surfaces** of the **cylindrical holes** at **each end of the beam.**

13.   **Radial > Fixed**

14.   **Axial > Fixed**

15.   **Tangential > Free** (See the next figure.)

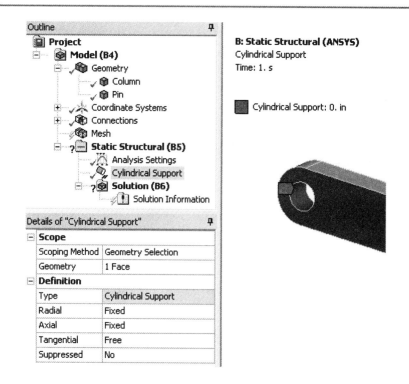

Figure 9-41 Cylindrical support.

On the right end set the contact between the pin and hole to be No Separation.

4.   Contact > Contact Region > Type > No Separation

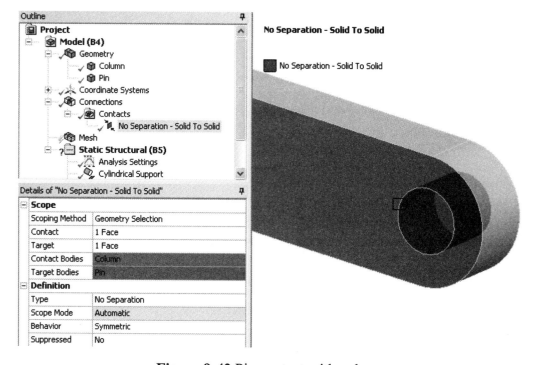

Figure 9-42 Pin contact with column.

5.   Double Click or **Drag Static Structural Analysis** to add it to the **Project.**

Apply loads and boundary conditions to the **near** and **far side faces of the pin: Unit load** in the **negative X Direction**, **No displacement** in the **Y or Z Direction**.

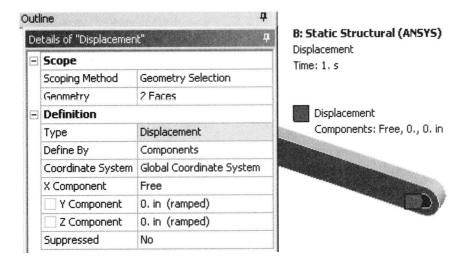

Figure 9-43 Displacement constraints applied to front and back of pin.

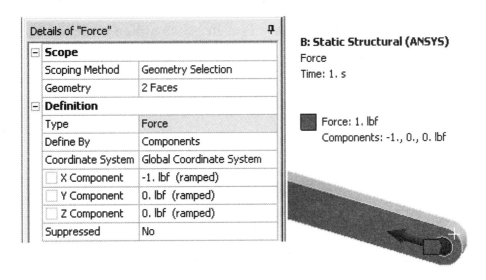

Figure 9-44 Loading applied to front and back of pin.

We need yet another constraint applied to the column to keep it from moving in the Z Direction. **Hide the pin** and apply a cylindrical constraint to the hole on the right end.

6.   Environment > Supports > Cylindrical Support

7.   Ctrl Select the Inside surfaces of the **cylindrical holes** at **each end of the beam.**

8.   Radial > Free

9.   **Axial > Fixed**

10.   **Tangential > Free** (See the next figure.)

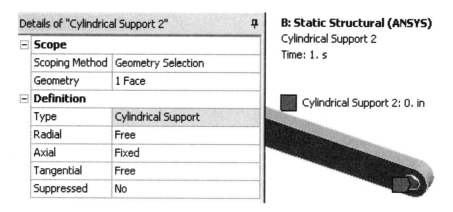

Figure 9-45 Cylindrical support to prevent Z-Direction movement.

16.   Add **Total Deformation** and **Normal Stress** in the **X-Direction** to the **Solution**

17.   Set the mesh element size to 0.5 inch, **Solve** :≶ Solve .

18.   **Right Click** on cell **B6 Solution > Transfer Data** to **New > Linear Buckling**

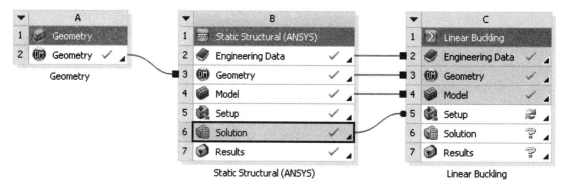

Figure 9-46 Transfer Data to Linear Buckling.

In linear buckling request that **two modes** be computed; the first mode is a **fixed-fixed XZ Plane mode**, and the second is the **pinned-pinned XY Plane mode** as shown below. (Pick two horizontal viewports.) Both elastic buckling loads are just over 19,000 lbf. This coincidence occurs because of different flexural inertias in the two planes combined with the different boundary conditions in the two planes of buckling.

Figure 9-47 Fixed-fixed and Pinned-pinned column modes.

Once again the computed results can be verified using column theory from solid mechanics. **Save your work.**

9-9   TUTORIAL 9F – BUCKLING OF A BUILT-UP STRUCTURE

The final example in this chapter considers the determination of the buckling load estimate for the built-up structure shown in the figures below. The utility of finite element methods is evident for problems such as this one. It is a component of a truck dumping mechanism that is placed in compression when in service and is constructed by welding simple structural shapes together to produce the end result depicted. The construct is shown in two stages.

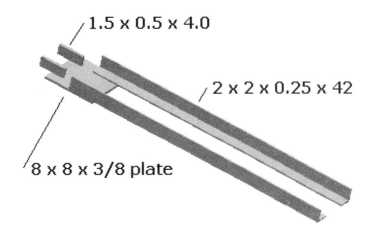

Figure 9-48 First stage of build up.

The left ends of the angle sections are placed at the center of the plate. The rectangular bars protrude 2 inches from the plate and are separated by 2 inches. The 0.25 x 2 x 8 braces shown below are equally spaced; the holes are centered 0.75 from the edges.

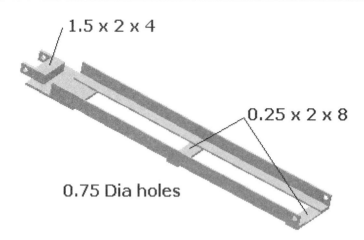

1.5 x 2 x 4

0.25 x 2 x 8

0.75 Dia holes

Figure 9-49 Second stage of build up.

As in Tutorial 9E above, we create an assembly that adds a **0.75 x 8 inch pin** at the right end to facilitate application of the boundary conditions.

1.   **Start ANSYS Workbench; Open the assembly** in **DesignModeler.** Check the units.

2.   **Accept the default structural steel.**

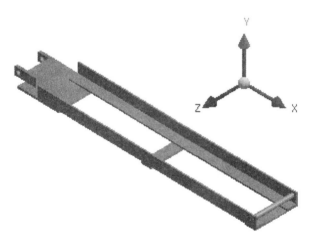

Figure 9-50 Pin-structure assembly.

Set the **pin-frame** contact characteristics

3.   **Contact > Contact Region > Type > No Separation**

Insert a new analysis

4.   **Add Static Structural Analysis**

Set a cylindrical support condition for the bore on the left end.

5.   Environment > Structural > Cylindrical Support

6.   Ctrl Select the Inside surfaces of the cylindrical holes at the left end.

7.   Radial > Fixed, Axial > Fixed, Tangential > Free

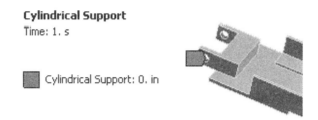

Figure 9-51 Cylindrical support.

8.   Apply loads and boundary conditions to both end faces of the pin: Unit load in the **negative X Direction, No displacement** in the **Y Direction.**

The labels only show on one end of the pin but be sure to Ctrl-select both faces.

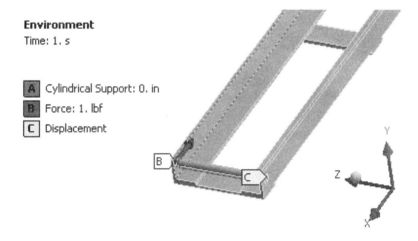

Figure 9-52 Loads and boundary condition at right end.

Proceed as in the previous tutorial.

Solve Structural Static Analysis for the Total Deformation. Set the element **mesh size to 0.5 inch** and Preview the mesh before solving.

9.   Mesh > Advanced > Element Size > 0.5 > Generate Mesh, Solve ⇒ Solve

Insert a buckling calculation object in the solution.

10.   Right Click Solution > Transfer Data to New Linear Buckling

11.   Linear Buckling > Max Modes to Find > 1; Solve ⚡Solve

The first mode of buckling is shown in the next illustration. The corresponding buckling load is about 71,000 lbf.

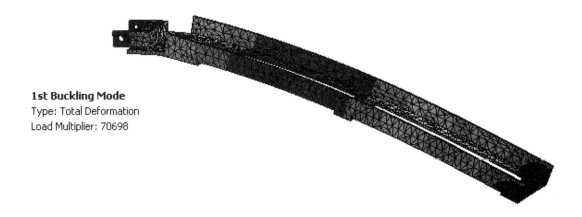

1st Buckling Mode
Type: Total Deformation
Load Multiplier: 70698

Figure 9-53 Buckling of the built-up frame.

Turn on the mesh display (show elements) and use animation to examine the deformation more closely, and you can observe the frame moving with respect to the pin.

The Euler buckling load for a pinned-pinned steel column 42 inches long with a cross section equivalent to two 2 x 2 x 0.25 angles is around 117,000 lbf, so the above result seems reasonable taking into account the thin plate at the left end.

9-10 SUMMARY

Chapter 9 presents tutorials illustrating the computation of natural frequencies and buckling loads for structural parts and assemblies. We note that the results can be substantially influenced by the quality of the mesh and it is recommended that some **mesh refinement** exploration be conducted before final results are accepted. Alternatively a convergence object can be inserted as we saw in Chapter 4.

Small local features such as holes and rounds were not included in our models here since they usually have little effect on frequency and buckling results which are usually global in nature.
Finally note that **buckling load estimates** are just that, estimates. The results computed here are based on perfectly straight, unblemished items with loads perfectly aligned. The actual situation is often much different.

In addition, the finite element shape function modeling process places an additional constraint on the deformation the mathematical model is allowed to experience. For these reasons elastic buckling loads as computed in this chapter are likely to be **non-conservative upper bounds** on the actual loads that may cause instability; that is, buckling may occur at a lower loading. An additional nonlinear analysis may be necessary to obtain a complete understanding of the real stability limits.

9-11   PROBLEMS

9-1   Compute the lowest **three natural frequencies** of an aluminum cantilever beam of the same dimensions as used in Tutorial 9A. Compare your results with values calculated using beam theory. Present your results in Rad/Sec, Hz, and RPM.

(Scc http://www.roymech.co.uk/Useful_Tables/Vibrations/Natural_Vibrations.html)

9-2   The steel cantilever beam below is 25 inches long and 0.25 inches wide. The left half has a cross section height of 1.0 inch and the right half a height of 0.5 inch. Find the lowest **three natural frequencies** of vibration. Sketch the mode shapes and describe in your words the type of motion that occurs in each. Present your frequency results in Rad/Sec, Hz, and RPM.

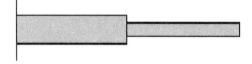

Figure P9-2

9-3   Find the **elastic buckling load** for a column such as used in Tutorial 9D but with **fixed-pinned** end conditions.

9-4   Compute the elastic buckling load for the beam of Problem 9-2.

9-5   An assembly of two identical bars 2.5 mm in width is shown below. One is made of steel, the other is made of copper alloy; they are bonded together to form a bimetallic strip. The left end is completely fixed. Find the lowest two natural frequencies of vibration. Sketch the mode shapes and describe in your words the type of motion that occurs in each. Present your frequency results in Rad/Sec, Hz, and RPM.

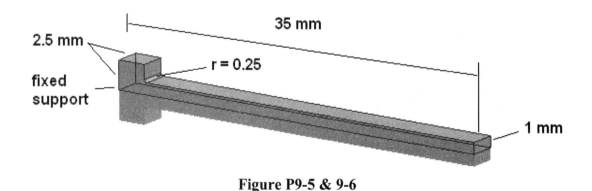

Figure P9-5 & 9-6

9-6   Find the axial compressive force that when applied the right end would cause elastic buckling of the beam in Problem 9-5.

9-7   Two 25 mm dia steel rods are joined to form a "T" part as shown. A 10 mm dia through hole and a 10 x 10 mm through hole are placed as shown. (The 65 mm dimension locates the left edge of the 10 x 10 hole.).

The left end is completely fixed. Find the lowest **three natural frequencies** of vibration. Sketch the mode shapes and describe in your words the type of motion that occurs in each. Present your frequency results in Rad/Sec, Hz, and RPM.

Use three different mesh densities corresponding to default sizes coarse, medium and fine. **Plot** the three calculated frequencies as a function of the number of elements in the mesh. How do your **results change** if you remove the two through hole features?

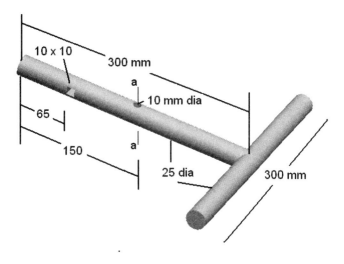

Figure P9-7

9-8   Find the **pressure** that causes **elastic buckling** of the cantilevered, structural steel beam shown. Submit a hand-drawn sketch to describe the buckled shape. Use a model with solid elements and another model with shell elements (see T8C and T9B).

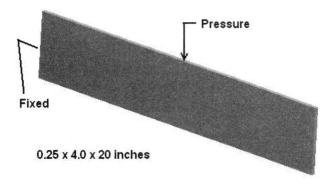

Figure P9-8 & 9-9

9-9 Find the lowest **three natural frequencies of vibration** of the 0.24 x 4.0 x 20 cantilever plate shown above. Submit a hand-drawn sketch to describe each mode. Use a model with solid elements and another model with shell elements (see T8C and T9B) compare your results.

REFERENCES

ANSYS Workbench

Peter Fröhlich, *FEM-Anwendungspraxis*, Friedr. Vieweg & Son Verlag GWV Fachverlage GmbH, 2005

Stefan Lecheler, *Numerische Stromungsberechnung*, Vieweg+Teubner, GWV Fachverlage GmbH, 2009

Huei-Huang Lee, *Finite Element Simulations with ANSYS Workbench 13*, Schroff Development Corporation, 2011.

Jack Zecher, Fereydoon Dadkhah, *ANSYS Workbench Tutorial with Multimedia CD Release 12*, Schroff Development Corporation, 2009

ANSYS APDL

Esam M. Alawadhi, *Finite Element Simulations Using ANSYS*, CRC Press, 2009, 416 pp.

Arshad Ali and Zeeshan Azmat, *Analysis of Composite Structure under Thermal Load Using ANSYS*, LAP Lambert Academic Publishing, 2010, 84 pp.

R.B. Choudary, *Introduction to Ansys 10.0*, I K International Publishing House, 2009, 128 pp.

Michael R. Hatch, *Vibration Simulation Using MATLAB and ANSYS*, Chapman and Hall/CRC, 2000, 654 pp.

Kent L Lawrence, *ANSYS Tutorial Release 13*, Schroff Development Corporation, 2011.

Erdogan Madenci, Ibrahim Guven, Bahattin Kilic, *Fatigue Life Prediction of Solder Joints in Electronic Packages with ANSYS*, The Springer International Series in Engineering and Computer Science, Springer, 2002, 208 pp.

Erdogan Madenci and Ibrahim Guven, *The Finite Element Method and Applications in Engineering Using ANSYS*, Springer, 2005, 686 pp.

Saeed Moaveni, *Finite Element Analysis Theory and Application with ANSYS*, 3rd Ed, Prentice Hall, 2007, 880 pp.

Tadeusz Stolarski and Y. Nakasone, *Engineering Analysis with ANSYS Software*, Butterworth-Heinemann , 2007, 480 pp.

Sham Tickoo, *ANSYS 11.0 for Designers*, CADCIM Technologies, 2009, 544 pp.

A number of web sites and online videos devoted to ANSYS Workbench and ANSYS APDL are also available.

NOTES: